FRENCH
Cookbook

Carol Liu
78.4.

Previous page: Kitchen herbs and a selection of French cooking equipment (see details on pages 11-2)

Opposite: Quiche Lorraine (see recipe on page 22).

FRENCH
Cookbook
Suzanne Gibbs

HG

Paul Hamlyn
Sydney London New York Toronto

Published by Paul Hamlyn Pty Ltd
176 South Creek Road, Dee Why West. NSW 2099
First published 1974
©Paul Hamlyn Pty Ltd 1974
National Library of Australia card number
and ISBN O 6OO O7326 2
Produced in Australia by the publisher
Typeset in Australia by Phototype–Sales
Printed in Hong Kong
PHOTOGRAPHER Reg Morrison
DESIGNER Helen Lesnewski
EDITOR Judith Dine
Line drawings by Ann Twells

Contents

Introduction

I am a very lucky person. I've always been surrounded by good food. I grew up in a small fishing village on the east coast of Australia, where the Hawkesbury River and the sea provided us with an abundance of fish, such things as asparagus grew wild and we had our own oyster lease. We raised ducks, geese and chickens, our garden boasted fruit trees, we grew our own vegetables and fresh cream and milk came from the two pet goats. We were self sufficient and lived on what could only be called the best in the land. My mother is a naturally fine cook which she says stems from her mother's Scottish cooking (very similar to the French home cooking). We shared the property with my aunt and her author husband who had returned from living many years in France and Italy. In this literary household everyone was genuinely interested in, and had a love for, good food.

It was while my mother was writing her first cookbook that I too began to cook seriously. Simple grills and salads at first, but I had learnt that the griller must be heated before adding the meat, I knew too that the salad greens must be washed and dried well and that freshly made oil and vinegar dressing should only be added at the last moment. My interest grew and I was soon off to the Cordon Bleu School of Cookery in London. I loved every minute of it and discovered that my early life on the Hawkesbury River could well have been a fishing village in France. Not surprising perhaps because my mother being a Scot had often spoken of the 'Auld Alliance'.

Fortunately, I am married to a man whose boyhood ambition was to marry a Cordon Bleu cook. So I have a responsive diner which is enough to urge any cook on. We eat simply, the way I always have. I like to feel that each meal is something special with loving effort put into it. We share a carafe of wine, and relax as we talk about the day's activities.

The French have inspired the world with their cooking, not only for great dishes but for the daily habit of eating well. I hope this **French Cookbook** will inspire you to do likewise.

Suzanne Gibbs

Guide to Weights and Measures

These tables are based on recommendations of the Metric Conversion Board to enable conversion between the imperial and the metric standard cooking measures of the Standards Association of Australia.

Note: For successful cooking either use metric weights and measures OR imperial weights and measures – do not use a mixture of the two.

LIQUID AND DRY MEASURES (volume)

Taking 1 imperial cup as equivalent to 1 metric cup this table provides a guide to convert volume measure in recipes.

	IMPERIAL	METRIC	
LIQUID (fl oz)=	IMPERIAL CUP –	METRIC CUP=	LIQUID
1 oz			30 ml
2 oz	¼ cup	¼ cup	
	⅓ cup	⅓ cup	
3 oz			100 ml
4 oz	½ cup	½ cup	
5 oz (¼ pint)	⅔ cup	⅔ cup	150 ml
6 oz	¾ cup	¾ cup	
8 oz	1 cup	1 cup	
10 oz (½ pint)	1¼ cups	1¼ cups	
12 oz	1½ cups	1½ cups	
15 oz (¾ pint)			475 ml
16 oz	2 cups	2 cups	
20 oz (1 pint)	2½ cups	2½ cups	

ABBREVIATIONS

kilogram	kg
gram	g
millilitre	ml
centimetre	cm
millimetre	mm

IMPERIAL TO METRIC (weights)

Taking 250 g as equivalent to 8 oz this table provides a guide to convert weight in recipes.

Ounces	Grams	Ounces	Grams
½ oz	15 g	11 oz	345 g
1 oz	30 g	12 oz (¾ lb)	375 g
2 oz	60 g	13 oz	410 g
3 oz	90 g	14 oz	440 g
4 oz (¼ lb)	125 g	15 oz	470 g
5 oz	155 g	16 oz (1 lb)	500 g (0.5 kg)
6 oz	185 g	24 oz (1½ lb)	750 g
7 oz	220 g	32 oz (2 lb)	1000 g (1 kg)
8 oz (½ lb)	250 g	3 lb	1500 g (1.5 kg)
9 oz	280 g	4 lb	2000 g (2 kg)
10 oz	315 g		

LENGTH

Millimetres/ Centimetres	Inches
3 mm	⅛ in
6 mm	¼ in
12 mm (1.2 cm)	½ in
20 mm (2 cm)	¾ in
25 mm (2.5 cm)	1 in
40 mm (4 cm)	1½ in
5 cm	2 in
6.5 cm	2½ in
8 cm	3 in
10 cm	4 in
13 cm	5 in
15 cm	6 in
18 cm	7 in
20.5 cm	8 in
23 cm	9 in
25.5 cm	10 in
28 cm	11 in
30.5 cm	12 in

OVEN TEMPERATURE GUIDE

THERMOSTAT SETTING

DESCRIPTION OF OVEN	ELECTRIC °F	°C	GAS °F	°C
Cool	200	110	200	100
Very slow	250	120	250	120
Slow	300	150	300	150
Moderately slow	350	180	325	160
Moderate	400	200	350	180
Moderately hot	425	220	375	190
Hot	450	230	400	200
Very hot	475	250	450	230

Equipment

Being able to call upon the right piece of equipment makes cooking a joy and not one of those dreadful tasks usually associated with housekeeping. More and more kitchen shops are opening and supplying us with the imported goods that make all the difference. Because good cooking is so important in France it is not surprising that most of this equipment is French, although their good designs are now being copied, which makes them considerably cheaper here. A suggestion though is to gradually build up a supply of good kitchen equipment; as you learn to cook with them you will have more idea of what you need.

Identification for photograph on page 1 (From the top, r to l.)

- These 2 brown fireproof dishes are the French style oven-to-tableware. They are made by Pillyuvet and are attractive for serving even if the food hasn't been cooked in them.
- The tiny mousse pots come in brown and white, they are used for baking petit pots de crème, or for individual mousses.
- This is basically a terrine mould, these come in round and oblong shapes and many sizes. Ideal for pâtés, or for serving vegetables and pickles.
- These fireproof white dishes are handy. Crudités (see page 116) look colourful in them, also good for serving hors d'oeuvre, individual side salads and vegetable entrées.
- Knives are perhaps the most important tools in the kitchen, so it is important to have good quality ones. The 'Sebatier' is one of the best on the market, and for a sharper edge choose carbon steel. The stainless steel knives are easier to clean, but are not as flexible and are harder to sharpen. For a good selection buy a metal spatula for pastries and cakes, a thick heavy knife for chopping and slicing, a long thin knife for carving, a small paring knife for little jobs, and a small stainless serrated knife for preparing fruits. The carbon steel knives are best cleaned with sandsoap and water, and for sharpening nothing beats a carbon stone. 'Johnson Overalls' in George St., Sydney, have a good selection, in the other states try the main department stores and the specialty kitchenware shops.

- A fine sieve for pastries and cakes, a help to baking enthusiasts.
- A mouli-sieve is one of the handiest pieces to have. These are easy to get, chemists and hardware shops have them. They are good for making puréed soups, and for potato and other vegetable purées.
- A wooden spoon for stirring sauces and beating butter cakes. Don't use it to stir foods containing onion, garlic or spices, as these flavours are easily picked up and impregnate the wood. The spoon with the hole is for beating special butter sauces.
- The tiny brush is for the pastry cooks; use it for brushing off excess flour, or brushing on glazes and beaten egg. One brush can be kept for brushing oil, melted butter or spicy seasonings on food.
- The little sauce whisk prevents lumps forming and is good for a curdled egg sauce. Use for whipping cream in preference to a rotary whisk which can easily turn cream to butter.
- A birch whisk is specifically for French dressing. After a few uses it becomes seasoned and shouldn't be used for mixing other foods.
- These heavy flan rings are for making tarts. Place directly on the baking sheet before lining with the pastry.
- A copper bowl is really the only thing worthy of beating egg whites. A greater volume is achieved, and a better quality for soufflés and meringues. A balloon whisk to fit the bowl is needed.
- These copper saucepans are French, and very expensive, as is all good copper. Clean the outside by rubbing with lemon juice or vinegar and salt.

Egg and Cheese Dishes

The French have a way with eggs. Eggs do not appear on the breakfast table as they do in Anglo-Saxon countries – in France piping hot café-au-lait and croissant, still warm from the baker's oven, is considered the only civilized way to start a day. But if an egg is not the way to start the day in France it certainly is popular from lunchtime onwards.

Eggs come in numerous guises in French cooking. Prepared in the stylish haute cuisine of a Paris restaurant, poached eggs may appear with pâté de foie gras on fried croûtes of bread, garnished with thin slices of truffle and coated with a fine sauce, or they may be set in aspic delicately flavoured and perfectly clear.

In the home, delicious little dishes come to the table; individual servings of eggs gently baked in cream and butter, often with a surprise flavouring, or as a golden omelette fragrant with herbs picked from the kitchen garden.

Here is a handful of simple egg dishes to serve as an entrée to a light meal or as a luncheon dish served with a crisp salad. Remember eggs are filling, and although simple, they can be very rich.

Cheese too is so much a part of the French way of life. Anyone who has visited France will have happy memories of simple meals taken with long batons of crusty bread, a selection of fine cheeses and a glass of wine. The best French cheeses have to be eaten on the spot but those that do travel to the corners of the world are often used in the preparation of many great cheese dishes – for instance, tiny Roquefort tartlets, served straight from the oven, or the inimitable Soufflé au Fromage.

Omelettes

There's no trick to making a good omelette. It is a matter of a little practice, choosing fresh eggs and most important – being meticulous about the pan. It should be heavy, well-oiled, without ever having been washed.

A new omelette pan needs to be seasoned. Three-quarters fill the pan with oil and add a teaspoon of salt. Bring to a gentle simmer, there should be the slightest movement on the surface of the oil. Remove from the heat and leave overnight. Pour off oil and with a cloth rub the salt into the pan to give it a good clean. From now on, after every use the pan should be cleaned with a little salt and the oiled cloth. After a while the pan will be reliable and produce a good omelette every time.

It is also important to keep the pan for cooking nothing but omelettes and pancakes. If other foods are cooked in it the seasoning will be lost. A good pan to choose when buying is one made of cast iron, for it is heavy, gives an even temperature and prevents burning.

French omelette
(Basic recipe)

3 eggs
salt and freshly ground pepper
1 tablespoon water
15 g (½ oz) butter

Serves: 1
Cooking time: 2 minutes

Break eggs into a bowl and beat lightly with a fork just to combine the whites with the yolks. It is important not to over-whisk for it makes the omelette tough. Add the seasonings and the water.

Melt half the butter in a frying pan and when the foam has subsided pour in the beaten eggs.

Using a fork or a metal spatula pull the egg mixture from the edge towards the centre allowing the uncooked mixture to run to the outside. Do this until the eggs have begun to set and the omelette is still quite soft.

Flip over one half of the omelette to the centre and flip over again so that the omelette is folded into three. Shake the omelette on to a heated plate. Melt remaining butter in pan and when it is sizzling pour over the omelette. Serve immediately.

Omelette aux fines herbes

Prepare a French omelette (see above) and sprinkle with freshly chopped mixed herbs before folding omelette. Parsley and chives are the herbs most often used but if you have chervil or basil add them as well.

Omelette au fromage

Prepare basic omelette recipe as follows:

Into the lightly beaten eggs stir 1 tablespoon of grated parmesan cheese. Season and stir in 2 teaspoons cream. Pour into the pan and sprinkle with 1 tablespoon finely diced cheese, preferably Gruyère or Emmenthaler. Cook as for French omelette (see opposite).

When cheese begins to melt fold over and serve immediately.

Omelette savoyarde

30 g (1 oz) butter
1 medium potato, diced
¼ cup diced lean bacon
¼ cup finely diced cheese
1 tablespoon chopped parsley

Filling: sufficient for 2 omelettes

Melt the butter in a pan and add potato. Cover and cook gently for about 8 minutes or until tender. Add bacon and continue cooking until fat is transparent.

Sprinkle cheese over eggs as soon as they are added to the pan. Spoon on potato and bacon and sprinkle with parsley just before folding. Fold and serve immediately.

Omelette piperade

1 small onion
3 tablespoons olive oil
2 tomatoes
2 peppers
1 small clove garlic
salt and freshly ground pepper
shredded basil, or
    pinch dried basil

Filling: sufficient for 4 omelettes

Peel, halve and chop the onion finely. Heat the olive oil in a pan and cook the onion until soft and light golden. Peel tomatoes and chop roughly. Wash and core peppers and cut into fine strips. Add to the pan with tomatoes and finely chopped garlic. Season and cook gently for about 15 minutes until the tomatoes and peppers are tender. Add a little shredded basil. Spoon over omelette before folding and serve immediately.

Boiled eggs

'Can't even boil an egg!' a comment sometimes passed about a cook, but it is so easy to become haphazard about this simple process. The choice of eggs, the speed of cooking and the timing all play an important part – and it is important. The hard-boiled egg has many uses in good French cooking. The white of a hard-boiled egg should be smooth and still fairly soft, the yolk cooked right through with no dark ring around the edge.

Use only very fresh eggs and at room temperature. Bring a pan of water to the boil, remove from heat and add eggs one by one, stirring with a metal spoon from side to side with a gently rolling action. This is to centre the yolk. Return the pan to heat and cook eggs at a gentle simmer for about 15 minutes. Remove eggs from pan and drop into a large bowl of iced water. This stops further cooking and prevents a dark edge forming around yolk.

To shell, lightly tap the eggs on a board and give a brisk roll under the hand, or tap the shell lightly, peel a strip around the centre of the egg and the two halves will slip off.

Many simple hors d'oeuvre, first course entrées and salads call for boiled eggs. Here are a few suggestions:

Oeufs mayonnaise: Arrange halved hard-boiled eggs on a bed of shredded lettuce or a crisp lettuce leaf, cut side down. Mask eggs with mayonnaise which has been thinned to a coating consistency with a little warm water. Decorate with strips of pimiento or a curled anchovy fillet. Sprinkle with chopped parsley.

Oeufs farci: Halve 6 hard-boiled eggs. Remove yolks and sieve into small bowl, beat in 3 tablespoons thick mayonnaise and 1 tablespoon softened butter.

To this can be added one of the following:
1 tablespoon finely chopped fresh herbs, 3 anchovy fillets pounded with a squeeze of lemon, 2 tablespoons chopped prawns with a squeeze of lemon and a pinch of nutmeg, 2 tablespoons good quality liver paste.

Arrange whites on serving dish and spoon a little stuffing into each.

Oeufs au cresson

(Eggs with watercress mayonnaise)

4 hard-boiled eggs
30 g (1 oz) butter
½ cup thick mayonnaise
2 teaspoons lemon juice
pinch cayenne pepper
salt
1 bunch watercress
1-2 tablespoons french dressing

Serves:4

Cut the eggs in half lengthwise, remove the yolks and rub through a sieve. Drop the whites into a bowl of cold water. Beat butter in a bowl until softened and beat in the sieved egg-yolks with 1 teaspoon of mayonnaise.

Season with the lemon juice and cayenne pepper and a pinch of salt. Trim much of the stalk from the watercress and blanch half in plenty of boiling water for 5 minutes. Drain, refresh under cold water and press to remove excess liquid.

Rub through a coarse sieve or purée in a blender. Add to the mayonnaise with a squeeze of lemon juice. Chop the remaining watercress very finely, leaving a bouquet aside for decoration. Spoon chopped watercress down the centre of a serving platter.

Dry the egg-whites, fill one with the yolk mixture and top with the other to re-shape into whole eggs. Arrange on watercress and coat each with the mayonnaise. Decorate with the bouquet of watercress and serve chilled.

Note: This is a delicious first course or luncheon dish.

Oeufs duxelles

(Gratin of eggs with mushrooms)

3 shallots
125 g (4 oz) mushrooms
30 g (1 oz) butter
1 tablespoon chopped mixed herbs
6 hard-boiled eggs
1 quantity béchamel sauce (see page 110)
salt and pepper
60 g (2 oz) grated cheese

Serves: 4-6
Cooking time: 10 minutes
Oven temperature: 170°C (350°F)

Chop shallots finely including a little of the green tops. Wipe mushrooms with a damp cloth and chop very finely. Melt butter in a pan and cook shallots and mushrooms over a gentle heat for about 5 minutes, add herbs.

Halve eggs and remove yolks, place whites in cold water. Sieve yolks into a bowl and add 2 tablespoons béchamel sauce. Beat until smooth and season to taste with salt and pepper. Spoon mushroom mixture down the centre of a shallow casserole. Arrange drained egg whites on top and spoon yolk mixture into each.

Beat grated cheese into remaining béchamel sauce and re-heat gently. Coat each egg with the sauce. Place in a preheated moderate oven for 10 minutes or until golden. Serve immediately.

A collection of delicious pâtés and terrines (see details on pages 45-8).

Oeufs en cocotte
(Baked eggs in ramekins)

These baked eggs are cooked very gently in a bain-marie (pan of water) in the oven. The eggs should remain soft and creamy without any crust. If you do not have small individual ramekins cook several eggs in a shallow casserole. This dish is ideal for serving at brunch or for a light luncheon.

butter
4 eggs
½ cup cream
a grinding of white pepper

Serves: 4
Cooking time: 8 minutes
Oven temperature: 170°C (350°F)

Butter 4 small ramekins and place in a roasting pan quarter filled with boiling water. Heat and drop an egg into each dish. Season cream with pepper to taste and pour over eggs. Top with a nut of butter and cover the pan with a sheet of buttered greaseproof paper. Bake in a preheated moderate oven for about 8 minutes or until just set. They are best when served immediately, sprinkled with a pinch of salt.

   This basic recipe lends itself to many variations using fresh ingredients on hand. A spoonful of any one of the following combinations can be placed on the bottom of each ramekin.

Aux duxelles: A good spoonful of the duxelles mixture which is used as a base for Coquilles à la Parisienne (see page 90).

Aux fines herbes: A classical garnish for eggs in France. Use a good sprinkling of freshly chopped parsley, chives, chervil and tarragon. The latter two are optional as they are not often on hand.

Aux épinards: For a first course or a light luncheon spinach partners very well with these eggs. Place a spoonful of cooked, finely chopped and buttered spinach or sorrel seasoned with freshly ground pepper in each ramekin.

Terrine maison (see recipe on page 47).

Quiche Lorraine

(See photograph on page 2.)

There has been much talk about the true Lorraine recipe for quiche. This is a very old recipe, using only cream and eggs, which the region produces in abundance. It seems natural that their famous quiche is simply a savoury custard tart.

Pastry:
1 cup plain flour
pinch salt
60 g (2 oz) butter
1 egg yolk
2 tablespoons iced water

Serves: 6
Cooking time: 35 minutes
Oven temperature: 190ºC (375ºF)

Filling:
60 g (2 oz) butter
1 cup cream
3 eggs
salt

Sift flour and salt into a bowl. Cut butter into small pieces and rub into flour. Combine egg yolk with water and use a knife to stir into flour mixture. Gather together to form a dough. Knead lightly, wrap and chill for at least 1 hour.

Place on to a floured surface and roll out to line a 20 cm (8 in) flan ring. Place on baking sheet and prick the bottom with a fork. Line pastry with a small piece of soft greaseproof paper and fill with dried beans. Chill for a further 15 minutes. Bake in a preheated moderately hot oven for 10 minutes. Remove beans and allow to cool.

Meanwhile cut butter into small pieces and place in base of pastry flan. Beat eggs with salt and stir in cream. Pour filling into pastry flan and continue to cook for a further 25 minutes, or until custard is set.

Note: This dish is delicious served hot with a fresh green salad, also goes well eaten cold.

Tarte aux oignons

(Onion tart)

Pastry:
1½ cups plain flour
pinch salt
125 g (4 oz) butter
1 egg yolk
3 tblspns iced water
dried beans

Filling:
2 large onions
125 g (4 oz) butter
1 tablespoon plain flour
3 eggs
⅔ cup cream
⅔ cup milk
salt and freshly ground pepper
pinch grated nutmeg

Serves: 6
Cooking time: 40 minutes
Oven temperature: 190ºC (375ºF)
lower to: 160ºC (325ºF)

First make the pastry. Sift the flour with the salt into a bowl. Cut the butter into small pieces and rub it into the flour until it resembles breadcrumbs. Combine the egg yolk with the water and blend into the flour mixture to form a dough. Knead lightly, wrap and chill for at least 1 hour.

Roll out thinly to line a 25.5 cm (10 in) flan ring or pie dish. Trim the edges and prick the base with a fork. Line pastry with a small piece of soft greaseproof paper and fill with dried beans. Chill for a further 15 minutes and bake in a preheated moderately hot oven for 10 minutes. Cool. Remove beans.

Meanwhile prepare the filling. Halve onions, peel and slice thinly. Melt butter in a heavy frying pan and cook onions until soft and almost cooked to a purée without colouring, about 15 minutes. Cool and combine with remaining ingredients. Season to taste with salt, pepper and nutmeg. Pour into pastry case and bake in a preheated moderately slow oven for 25 minutes. Serve very hot.

Soufflé au fromage

(Cheese soufflé)

dried toasted breadcrumbs
45 g (1½ oz) butter
30 g (1 oz) plain flour
1 cup milk
4 egg yolks
45 g (1½ oz) grated Parmesan cheese
45 g (½ oz) finely diced Gruyère or
   Emmenthaler
salt
pinch cayenne pepper
5 egg whites

Serves: 4-6
Cooking time: 25 minutes
Oven temperature: 190°C (375°F)

Fold a sheet of greaseproof paper in half. Turn a 2.5 cm (1 in) rim on the folded edge. Butter a size 1 soufflé dish and tie the band of greaseproof (folded edge on the bottom) around the outside with string. Butter the inside of the band. Shake the breadcrumbs inside the dish reserving a few to sprinkle on the top.

Melt the butter in a saucepan and blend in flour. Draw aside and add milk. Return to heat and stir continuously until it is boiling and has formed a thick white sauce. Allow to cool slightly and beat in the egg yolks, seasonings and cheeses.

Clean a copper bowl with lemon juice and salt or use a white china bowl. Add egg whites and whisk until stiff and dry. Lightly stir a spoonful of the egg whites into the cheese sauce and fold in remaining egg whites quickly and gently.

Pour into the prepared soufflé dish. Work a knife around the edge of the souf-flé and in the centre to form a small circle to give the soufflé a 'cap'. Sprinkle with the breadcrumbs and a little extra Parmesan cheese. Place on a heated baking sheet and bake in a preheated moderately hot oven for 25 minutes or until a good golden colour.

Remove from oven and place directly on a heated plate. Remove the band and string and serve soufflé immediately, using a large spoon to break the top and scoop from the bottom of the soufflé.

Once you are familiar with this basic recipe it is a simple matter to prepare various soufflés with the addition of other flavours. There is always the makings of a soufflé in the pantry and with small leftovers of some fine flavoured dish in the refrigerator.

Shellfish soufflé: Prepare cheese soufflé mixture (see above), add to prepared soufflé dish in alternate layers with 1 cup chopped prawns, crab-meat or lobster, which has been tossed in 1 tablespoon butter over a brisk heat and flamed with 1 tablespoon warmed brandy or whisky. Bake as for cheese soufflé.

Mushroom soufflé: Sauté 1 cup sliced button mushrooms in 1 tablespoon butter for 1-2 minutes. Sprinkle with 1 tablespoon chopped mixed herbs (parsley, chives and a little marjoram). Add to cheese sauce mixture before folding in egg whites. Bake as for cheese soufflé.

Zucchini soufflé: Trim and slice tiny zucchini. Cook in a little butter until tender. Season with salt and pepper. Spoon into base of prepared soufflé dish, top with cheese soufflé mixture. Bake as for cheese soufflé.

Soufflé d'épinards au jambon
(Spinach and ham soufflé)

250 g (8 oz) packet frozen spinach
15 g (½ oz) butter
2 teaspoons plain flour
⅓ cup cream
2 egg yolks
salt and freshly ground pepper
pinch grated nutmeg
60 g (2 oz) ham, finely diced
4 egg whites

Serves: 4-6
Cooking time: 25 minutes
Oven temperature: 190°C (375°F)

Prepare a size 1 soufflé dish as for cheese soufflé. Heat the spinach according to the directions on the packet with the butter and allow to cook briskly to evaporate excess liquid. Stir in the flour, cook 1 minute and blend in the cream. Bring to the boil. Remove from heat, cool slightly then beat in egg yolks and seasonings. Add the ham.

Beat the egg whites until stiff, stir a spoonful into the spinach mixture and fold in remainder quickly and lightly. Pour into prepared soufflé dish and bake for 25 minutes in a preheated moderately hot oven. Place on a heated plate, remove band and string and serve immediately.

Roquefort tartlets

Pastry:
1 cup plain flour
90 g (3 oz) butter
1 egg yolk
2 tablespoons iced water

Filling:
15 g (½ oz) butter
1 tablespoon plain flour
⅔ cup milk
⅔ cup cream
125 g (4 oz) Roquefort cheese
3 egg yolks

Cooking time: 25 minutes
Oven temperature: 190°C (375°F)
lower to: 170°C (350°F)

Sift flour with a pinch of salt into a bowl. Cut butter into small pieces and rub into flour until mixture resembles breadcrumbs. Combine egg yolk with water and add to flour to form a dough. Knead lightly, wrap and chill for at least 1 hour. Roll out thinly and line small tartlet tins.

Trim edges and prick each base. Chill for a further 15 minutes. Bake in a preheated moderately hot oven for 5 minutes.

Meanwhile prepare filling. Melt butter in a small saucepan, draw aside and add flour. Blend until smooth and add milk. Bring to the boil stirring constantly. Add the cream and simmer for a few minutes. Grate the Roquefort cheese and add to cream sauce with the egg yolks. Pour into tartlet cases and place in preheated moderate oven for 20 minutes. Serve hot.

Feuilletées Roquefort

250 g (8 oz) puff pastry
250 g (8 oz) Roquefort cheese
1 egg, beaten

Cooking time: 15-20 minutes
Oven temperature: 200°C (400°F)

Roll the pastry on a floured surface to a rectangle 30.5 cm x 20 cm (12 in x 8 in) and cut into 2 pieces. Dampen the edges of one half. Cut the cheese into 8 fingers and lay over the pastry half at even intervals. Cover with the other pastry half, pressing down well between each piece of cheese. Cut between the cheese into fingers and place on a greased baking sheet. Brush lightly with beaten egg and bake in a preheated hot oven for 15-20 minutes or until golden and puffed. Serve hot.

Croque monsieur

These are fried cheese and ham sandwiches, often bought in Paris as we might buy a hamburger for a quick snack. They may also be served as a hors d'oeuvre.

Cut slices of white bread into 5 cm (2 in) squares. Cut slices of ham and Gruyère cheese the same size. Butter one side of the bread only, lay a slice of cheese on top and spread with a little French mustard, lay a slice of ham on this and top with another square of bread. Press down well and fry in a pan of sizzling butter until golden on both sides.

Cheese sablés

(Cheese biscuits)

Sift flour with a pinch of salt into a bowl. Cut butter into small pieces and rub into flour. Stir in cheese, season with pepper and gather to form a dough. Knead lightly, wrap and chill for at least 1 hour.

Roll out thinly to a rectangle and cut into 5 cm (2 in) strips. Cut each strip into triangles and place on a greased baking sheet. Brush with beaten egg and bake in a preheated moderately hot oven for 8-10 minutes or until golden and puffed. Ease sablés from baking sheet immediately and allow to cool.

Note. These go well with a glass of sherry. They are an excellent accompaniment to many light soups.

Crêpes

Crêpes are one of the specialities of French cooking. In this land of good cooks a pancake becomes a crêpe, paper-thin and round, resembling a fine lace doily. It can be eaten English-style with a squeeze of lemon and dusting of sugar, but more often its tender delicate form encloses some of the great treats of the French kitchen. Crêpes provide a cook with a wonderful repertoire of hot entrées and sweet dishes, the best known being that most heavenly of desserts Crêpes Suzette.

Crêpes aux crustacés

(Crêpes with shellfish)

16 basic crêpes
6 shallots, finely chopped
60 g (2 oz) butter
2 cups cooked shellfish
   (prawns, lobster and crabmeat)
2½ cups béchamel sauce (see page 110)
1 egg yolk
1 tablespoon dry sherry
1 tablespoon snipped chives
salt and pepper
¼ cup cream, whipped

Serves: 6-8
Cooking time: 15 minutes
Oven temperature: 170°C (350°F)

Sauté the shallots in butter until soft. Dice shellfish or if using crabmeat flake finely. Place in a bowl with the cooked shallots and half the béchamel sauce.

Add the egg yolk, sherry and chives and season to taste with salt and pepper.

Fill each crêpe with this mixture, roll up and lay in a buttered shallow casserole. Cover with foil or a piece of buttered greaseproof paper and bake in a preheated moderate oven for 15 minutes.

Reheat remaining béchamel sauce with the cream and spoon over each crêpe. Return to moderate oven for 8 minutes or until golden.

Note: Crêpes freeze well, so it is worthwhile cooking them ahead for an occasion. Stack with a small square of greaseproof between each crêpe. Wrap in foil or plastic. They also freeze well when filled, only requiring heating in the oven to serve.

Crêpes d'épinards

(Spinach filled crêpes)

16 fine crêpes
500 g (1 lb) spinach
15 g (½ oz) butter
1 tablespoon flour
salt and freshly ground pepper
pinch of grated nutmeg
2 tablespoons cream
30 g (1 oz) butter
2 tablespoons plain flour
1¼ cups milk
½ teaspoon French mustard

Serves: 6-8
Cooking time: 5 minutes
Oven temperature: 190ºC (375ºF)

Make the crêpes and keep warm while preparing filling and cooking sauce.

Wash and trim spinach and cook in 1 tablespoon water until tender, about 5 minutes.

Drain and press the liquid from spinach. Chop finely and return to pan with 15 g (½ oz) of the butter. Blend in the flour with the seasonings and cream. Stir well over a brisk heat until creamy and well blended.

Fill each crêpe with the spinach mixture and roll into a cigar shape. Arrange on a buttered fireproof shallow serving dish.

Melt remaining butter in a pan and blend in remaining flour. Stir in the milk, blending well. Bring to the boil, stirring constantly and simmer for a few minutes to thicken. Check for seasoning with salt and freshly ground pepper, and mustard. Add half the Parmesan with the Gruyère cheese.

Coat each crêpe with the hot sauce and sprinkle with reserved Parmesan. Place in a preheated moderately hot oven for 5 minutes or until golden.

Crêpes au jambon

(Crêpes with ham)

16 crepes
375 g (12 oz) ham slices
2 cups cream
1 cup grated Gruyère cheese
30 g (1 oz) butter

Serves: 6-8
Cooking time: 15 minutes
Oven temperature:160°C (325°F)

Make the crêpes and stack on a hot plate. Have ready the ham slices cut into fine 2.5 cm (1 in) strips and use to fill each crêpe.

Roll the crêpes into a cigar shape and arrange in a buttered, shallow dish. Pour the cream over and sprinkle with the cheese. Dot with the butter and bake in a preheated moderately slow oven for 15 minutes or until golden.

Crêpes

1¼ cups plain flour
pinch salt
3 eggs, beaten
1½ cups milk
1 tablespoon brandy
2 teaspoons melted butter
extra butter

Makes about
20 fine crêpes

Sift flour with salt into a mixing bowl. Make a well in the centre and add eggs and milk. With a wooden spoon gradually draw in the flour. Beat well and stir in the brandy and melted butter. Cover and leave to stand for 1 hour.

Heat a little butter in a heavy frying pan or special crêpe pan. Pour off excess, reserving for when pan needs re-greasing.

Use a soup ladle and pour enough batter to thinly coat surface of pan. Rotate the pan quickly and run the batter smoothly and evenly over the surface, pour off any excess batter. The crêpes should be about 13 cm (5 in) across.

Cook until small bubbles appear, about 1 minute, then use a metal spatula to flip the crêpe over. Cook 1 minute on the other side. Stack crêpes flat on a hot plate until they are all made.

Soups

'SOUP OF THE EVENING, BEAUTIFUL SOUP.' Tell me dear Alice, did your adventures in wonderland ever take you to France? Was Mock Turtle, as he sat by the sea and sang his little song, dreaming of the beautiful soups from across the channel? For anyone who has tasted the simple and the great French soups could burst into song at the very thought of them.

Many French people even start the day with a bowl of soup. Farmers and peasants, who rise with the sun, just heat up a bowl of broth often left over from the evening meal. Generations of Parisian theatre goers have taken night caps of French Onion Soup in the wee-small hours of the morning at Les Halles as the markets were opening to sell the fresh produce that would travel that day to kitchens the length and breadth of France.

The nicest thing about French soups to my way of thinking is that there are no definite rules for making them – providing the results are good. Great restaurants depend upon excellent basic stocks to produce the most superlative soups in the world, while an equally good if less magnificent broth may be simply a purée of potatoes and onions enriched with a spoonful of cream, an egg yolk or a knob of butter. The French are noted for their frugal ways, but this is turned to great advantage when one sees what a housewife can make from a few simple ingredients.

Included in this chapter are some of the soups of France which can be made easily from ingredients you may have on hand or can easily obtain – it is the little finishing touches that make them inimitably French.

Bouillon de boeuf

(Beef bouillon)

This simple soup is made several times a week in any household that enjoys a simple clear broth. The meat is often served with a dish of sea salt and a bowl of boiled or mashed potatoes.

1 kg (2 lb) shin of beef   Serves: 6
2 carrots
2 small turnips
2 leeks or onions
1 stalk celery
2.5 litres (4 pints) water
2 teaspoons salt
pepper
thyme, bay leaf

Wipe the meat with a damp cloth. Scrape carrots, quarter turnips, cut leeks in halves.

Place meat and vegetables in a large deep saucepan. Add the water and seasonings. Bring slowly to the boil and remove any scum, reduce heat, cover pan and simmer gently for 3 hours.

Strain the soup. The meat may be served separately with potatoes. The clear broth is served as bouillon or it may be used as stock for other soups.

Bouillon de poulet

(Chicken broth)

Like beef broth this is one of the simple soups of France. The fowl is often eaten with potatoes or cut up and served in the broth. The broth may be thickened if desired. Sometimes a handful of fresh young spring vegetables are chopped and added to the strained broth and cooked for a short while.

1 boiling fowl
2 carrots, sliced
1 turnip, quartered
2 leeks or onions, sliced
salt, pepper
bouquet garni (comprising thyme,
** bay leaf, celery)**
2.5 litres (4 pints) water

Serves: 6

Wipe the chicken and place in a large deep saucepan. Add vegetables, seasonings and water to cover, it may be necessary to add more water than quantity given above, depending largely on the size of the fowl.

Bring slowly to the boil and remove any scum that forms. Reduce heat, cover the pan and simmer gently until the fowl is tender, this will take from 1½ to 3 hours depending largely on size and age of bird.

Remove the chicken. Serve the soup with the vegetables or better still serve it this way:

Strain the soup. Reheat the stock, add 60 g (2 oz) tapioca or vermicelli and if liked, 1 cup of diced mixed vegetables. Simmer gently until vegetables are cooked and soup thickens, about 10 minutes.

If preferred omit the vegetables and tapioca and thicken the soup with a beaten egg, just add a little of the hot stock to beaten egg, blend, then stir into soup and serve at once.

If broth cooks down too much, as may happen during long cooking, add 1 or more cups of hot water for the last hour.

Potage crème aux champignons

(Cream of mushroom soup)
(See photograph opposite)

The full flavour of mushrooms is the feature of this beautiful cream soup. Open, flat mushrooms which have the best flavour are added raw to the hot soup base and puréed in an electric blender. No electric blender? Simply push the soup and sliced mushrooms through a coarse sieve or a mouli.

1 bunch shallots
60 g (2 oz) butter
1 clove garlic
salt and freshly ground pepper
3 tablespoons flour
4 cups chicken stock
250 g (8 oz) mushrooms
½ cup cream
chopped chives or mint

Serves: 4-6

Trim shallots and wash well. Slice shallots using the green part as well. Melt the butter in a deep saucepan, add the shallots and peeled clove of garlic. Cover pan and cook vegetables gently until they are quite soft. Season with salt and pepper. Blend in the flour and continue to stir over a low heat for a minute or two. Add the stock, stirring gently until soup comes to the boil and then simmer for 10 minutes.

Wipe the mushrooms with a damp cloth and slice. Combine a cup of warm soup with a handful of mushrooms and purée in an electric blender. Repeat with remaining soup and mushrooms.

Return the purée to the pan. Add the cream, reheat. Taste and correct seasoning if necessary. Serve hot or alternatively well chilled.

Note: An additional spoonful of cream may be swirled into soup, garnish with a sprinkling of snipped chives or tiny mint sprigs.

Potage crème aux champignons (Cream of mushroom soup).

Soupe au pistou
(Vegetable soup with basil)

(See photograph opposite)

This robust soup is loved in Provence although it is claimed to have originated in Genoa, the coastal town of Italy that looks across to the French coast. A hearty bean and vegetable soup it is thickened with pistou, the aromatic blend of oil, garlic, tomatoes and the pungent basil. As basil is so important to this soup (and many other dishes) it is worth growing this summer herb in quantities enough to put down for the winter months. Strip the leaves and pack in jars in a good olive oil. It will refrigerate for 6 months and while the leaves may discolour none of the flavour is lost.

500 g (1 lb) dried haricot beans   Serves: 6-8
1 large onion
500 g (1 lb) green beans
500 g (1 lb) zucchini
6 medium potatoes
30 g (1 oz) butter
3 litres (5 pints) water
2 teaspoons salt

Basil paste:
1 cup basil leaves
4 cloves garlic
2 large tomatoes
4 teaspoons tomato paste
125 g (4 oz) Gruyère cheese
3 tablespoons olive oil

Soak beans overnight. Place in saucepan and cover with fresh water. Bring to the boil, cover and simmer gently for 15 minutes, drain.

Chop onion finely. Trim beans and cut into 1.25 cm (½ in) lengths. Trim zucchini and cut into .5 cm (¼ in) slices. Peel potatoes and cut into 1.25 cm (½ in) dice.

Melt butter in a large deep pan and sauté prepared vegetables, including haricots, until softened, about 5 minutes. Cover with cold water and add salt. Cover and simmer gently for 1 hour. Break vermicelli into 2.5 cm (1 in) lengths and add to soup, cooking for about 15 minutes longer.

Meanwhile make basil paste and stir into soup just before serving. Serve hot with crusty bread.

Basil paste: Shred basil finely and place in a bowl with crushed garlic. Peel and chop tomatoes and add to basil with tomato paste and grated cheese. With a pestle or end of a rolling pin (a blender is also excellent for this) pound to a smooth paste. When smooth gradually add oil, beating well. Set aside to serve with soup.

Soupe au pistou (Vegetable soup with basil).

Potage aux concombres

(Cucumber soup, cold)

The perfect soup for a hot summery day, especially when the soft green of the cucumber is retained – the trick is to plunge the cucumber into boiling salted water and cook until just tender, thus preserving the fresh cool flavour.

5 medium cucumbers   Serves: 4-6
2 cups water
salt
1 teaspoon dried tarragon
salt and pepper
1 cup cream
paprika

Peel 4 cucumbers, using a swivel blade vegetable peeler, leaving a hint of the pale green colour under the cucumber skin. Cut cucumber into thick chunks.

Bring salted water to boil, drop in the cucumber and cook until tender.

Drain and force the cucumbers through a coarse sieve, or purée in a blender. You should have a thick liquid. Add the finely crumbled tarragon, season with salt and pepper, mix with the cream and chill in covered container in the refrigerator. Peel remaining cucumber, cut flesh into fine dice, drop into boiling salted water and cook for 3-4 minutes, drain and reserve for garnishing soup.

Before serving soup check for seasoning – food chilled often requires a little more salt than when freshly made. Serve in small bowls garnished with diced cooked cucumber and sprinkle with a little paprika.

Soupe au cresson

(Watercress soup)

Many fine French soups are based on the simple purée of boiled potatoes. One of the best is this watercress soup, the freshly chopped cress added just before serving with a minimum of cooking seems to retain the fresh spiciness of this admirable green.

3-4 medium potatoes
3 cups water
salt
3 cups milk
1 bunch watercress
30 g (1 oz) butter

Serves: 4

Peel the potatoes and cut into quarters. Put in a deep saucepan, cover with 3 cups water and boil gently, about 15-20 minutes or until tender. Do not strain but mash them in the saucepan. Season with salt.

Bring milk to a simmer and blend into the potatoes, the soup should be the consistency of cream.

Trim the stems from the watercress, break cress into little branches, wash well. Chop roughly, there should be about 1½ cups of leaves, and add to the soup, cook for 10 minutes. Just before serving stir in the butter or spoonful of cream and serve immediately.

Potage saint-germain

(Cream of green pea soup)

500 g (1 lb) fresh peas,
   or 1 packet frozen
30 g (1 oz) butter
1 small onion, quartered
sprig of mint and parsley
6 lettuce leaves, shredded
3 cups chicken stock or water
salt and pepper
½ cup cream

Serves: 4-6

Shell and rinse peas, wash a handful of the greenest shells. Melt butter in saucepan, add peas, shells, onion, mint and parsley, cover pan and cook very gently for 5 minutes. Add lettuce and stock and simmer gently until tender. Remove shells, parsley, mint and onion.

Push peas through sieve (or purée in electric blender) return to pan. Correct seasoning, if soup is too thick, as may happen if peas are a little old or if the purée has been made in the electric blender, it may be thinned with scalded milk. It should be the consistency of cream.

Let it simmer for 10 minutes and just before serving swirl in the cream.

Note: This soup may be served cold. If after chilling it thickens a little, just dilute with milk.

Soupe au potiron

(Pumpkin soup)

The cinderella pumpkin is transformed into a not so humble golden soup fit for any princely table. Its simple preparation, with just a hint of seasoning, is typical of French home cooking.

Note: Pumpkin soup does not improve on keeping, it is at its best when freshly made.

750 g (1½ lb) pumpkin   Serves: 4-6
1 small onion
water
2 teaspoons salt
2½ cups scalded milk
2 teaspoons sugar
salt, pepper and nutmeg
6 slices French bread

Peel the pumpkin and cut up roughly. Peel and quarter onion. Place in deep saucepan and just cover with water, add salt, bring to boil and cook until tender.

Force vegetables through a sieve and mix with the hot milk until it has the consistency of cream, or purée in electric blender with hot scalded milk. Season with sugar, salt and pepper and just a light sprinkling of nutmeg.

Place the bread in a soup tureen and pour soup over the bread. Allow to stand a few minutes before serving.

Variation: As an alternative way of serving this soup, omit the French bread and swirl a knob of butter or a few spoonsful of cream into the finished soup just before it is served, top with salted fried bread croûtons and a dusting of chopped parsley.

Potage purée de haricot rouges

(Red bean soup)

250 g (8 oz) red kidney beans
water
30 g (1 oz) butter
1 large onion, chopped
1 carrot, sliced
bouquet garni (comprising thyme,
    bay leaf, parsley)
½ cup red wine
2-3 teaspoons salt, pepper
1 tablespoon tomato paste
1.75 litres (3½ pints) stock
additional 15 g (½ oz) butter
croûtons of fried bread

Serves: 6

Soak the beans overnight in plenty of water, drain and rinse. Put in a large saucepan. Cook in water to cover, about 30 minutes. Drain and refresh under fresh water.

Melt butter in a deep pan, add onion and carrot and cook, covered, over a gentle heat for 4-5 minutes. Add the beans, bouquet garni, wine, salt, tomato paste and stock. Bring to the boil then reduce heat and simmer very gently until beans are soft, about 1 hour.

Push beans and vegetables through a sieve or mouli, or purée in an electric blender. Return to pan and taste for seasoning. The soup should have the consistency of thick cream, if too thick add more wine or stock. This is sometimes necessary when the soup is put through the electric blender, it seems to thicken many soups and purées.

Reheat to boiling point, add the butter. As soon as it melts serve with lightly salted croûtons.

Pâtés and terrines

(See photographs on pages 19-20)

Anyone who has been to France will remember with great nostalgia the magnificent pâtés and terrines. One can choose from an enormous selection of these delightful meats which are popular for simple luncheons eaten with the incomparable French crusty batons, a pat of fresh butter, and a glass of red wine. These meats are commonly made at home in France, each household has its own recipe, which is often called pâté maison.

If you find you have developed a taste for these well-flavoured dishes which require minced meat, it is certainly worth buying a small hand mincer.

Quatre épices, important to all pâtés and terrines, is a blend of four spices sold commercially in France. It is a simple matter to blend your own so I have included a recipe. They are ground easily in an electric blender. The juniper berry is the other seasoning that gives pâté an undeniably great flavour. These berries have to be imported and so are difficult to get in some areas, but a pinch of them ground does wonders to a basic recipe.

The terrine moulds are available in kitchen shops, and the terrines look good served straight from these earthenware or china dishes.

Terrines always have a lining of fat whether it be in the form of pork fat, bacon or clarified butter, which keep the meats moist for the 2 days the flavours are left to develop. They are cooked **au bain marie,** which simply means in a pan of water, this is to avoid shrinkage and flavour loss from high heat.

Note: It is important to discover a good pork butcher so that you have a reliable source of supply for pâtés and terrines. For people living in Sydney one of the best places to go for good quality fresh pork ingredients is the Yee Sing Butchery at 80 Harbour Street, Haymarket.

Quatre épices
(Four spices)

125 g (4 oz) white peppercorns
1 tablespoon whole cloves
35 g (1½ oz) nutmeg, coarsely
   chopped
30 g (1 oz) ground ginger

Grind the peppercorns, cloves and nutmeg in an electric blender to a fine powder. Combine well with the ground ginger and store in an airtight jar.

Rillettes de porc
(Shredded pork pâté)

1 kg (2 lb) pork belly   Serves: 4-6
1 large clove garlic
sprig thyme
salt and freshly ground pepper
pinch nutmeg

Remove the rind and small bones from the pork belly. Cut the meat into small pieces and place in a heavy pan with remaining ingredients. Cover and cook over a very gentle heat for 1½ hours or until pork is tender. Strain the fat from the pork and remove the thyme. Allow to cool.

Place the pieces of pork on a board and using 2 forks shred the meat finely. Pack tightly into small earthenware pots and cover with a round of foil. Place the lid on top and keep in the refrigerator. Serve with piping hot toast or fresh crusty bread.

Terrine maison

(See photograph on page 20)

1 thin slice pork fat, or 8 rashers
   streaky bacon
375 g (12 oz) pigs liver
1 small onion, peeled
1 clove garlic, peeled
375 g (12 oz) pork mince
2 teaspoons salt
large pinch quatre épices (see
   page 46)
1 tablespoon chopped parsley
250 g (8 oz) lean veal, diced finely
2 tablespoons brandy
bay leaf
½ cup plain flour
½ cup water

Serves: 6-8
Cooking time: 2 hours
Oven temperature: 180°C (350°F)

Ask the butcher to bat the pork fat out with a mallet. If using bacon rashers, line a small terrine with enough overhanging to fold on top of the filled terrine. Roughly chop the liver and mince with the onion and garlic. Place in a large bowl with the pork mince, seasonings, parsley, diced veal and brandy.

Fill the prepared terrine with this mixture and cover with the thinly sliced pork fat, or fold over the bacon. Top with the bay leaf, and cover with the lid. Combine flour and water, and use this paste to seal. Place in a pan of warm water and bake in a preheated moderate oven for 2 hours.

Take out, remove the lid and place a light weight on top (about 750 g (1½ lb)). This is for easier slicing. Leave for 2 days before eating to allow the flavours to develop. If liked, the day after baking, the terrine can be filled with a light jellied stock (see page 118).

Serve cut in thick slices with crusty bread and a pat of butter (preferably unsalted).

Note: This terrine can be served as an entrée or a light luncheon.

Pâté de poulet

(Chicken pâté)

thin slice of pork fat,
   or 8 rashers streaky bacon
250 g (8 oz) chicken breast
2 tablespoons brandy or Calvados
500 g (1 lb) chicken flesh
750 g (1½ lb) shoulder pork
3 teaspoons salt
large pinch quatre épices (see
   page 46)
large pinch crushed juniper berries
3 tablespoons chopped parsley
bay leaf
½ cup plain flour
½ cup water

Serves: 6
Cooking time: 2 hours
Oven temperature: 160°C (325°F)

Bat the pork fat out thinly or ask the butcher to do it for you. If using bacon rashers line a terrine with them. Shred the chicken breast finely and leave to marinate in the brandy while preparing meats.

Mince the chicken flesh and pork together and place in a large bowl. Season with the salt, spices and add the parsley. Pack half of this mixture in the terrine and top with the shredded chicken breast. Fill with remaining meat mixture and fold over the bacon rashers, or if using pork fat, lay it on top. Place a bay leaf in the centre and cover with the lid.

Make a paste with the flour and water and use to seal the edge of the lid. Place in a pan of water and bake in a preheated moderately slow oven for 2 hours. Remove from oven and cool slightly before removing the lid. Place a light weight on top and leave to cool before covering with foil and refrigerating.

Meat dishes

In their desire to use every piece of meat to its best advantage, the French have evolved recipes including the cheapest cuts of meat that have become world classics. Beefsteaks are well known to anyone who has eaten in France. Always of the prime cuts they can be entrecôtes which are taken from the ribs, or chateaubriand, which is the very eye of the fillet, tournedos from the middle or fillet mignon from the tail of the fillet. They are usually pan fried, the pan juices always being deglazed with brandy, wine or a swirl of cream for a special flavour.

The French never roast any but the best cuts of meat. These are served underdone, with a simple garnish and the pan juices left unthickened. But no less esteemed are the daubes and braises, so often put on in the morning and left simmering gently all day to fill the air with magnificent tempting aromas.

Steak au poivre

(Pepper steak)

Cans of green peppercorns are available in specialty kitchen shops and a few main department stores. These are excellent for this dish but without them the dried black peppercorns will do.

4 x 4 cm (1½ in) thick fillet steaks
olive oil
1 tablespoon coarsely cracked black
**   peppercorns**
30 g (1 oz) butter
2 tablespoons brandy
squeeze lemon juice
¼ cup cream
salt to taste

Serves: 4

Tie the steaks into neat round shapes with string. Brush with the oil and press the peppercorns into each. Leave for 1 hour.

Melt the butter in a heavy frying pan and when sizzling hot add the steaks. Cook over a brisk heat for 3-4 minutes on each side. Place on a heated serving dish and keep warm. Return the pan to the heat. Warm the brandy, set alight and add to pan. Shake the pan until flames subside and add lemon juice, cream and salt. Reheat and spoon over the steaks. Serve at once.

Filet de boeuf béarnaise

(Fillet of beef with béarnaise sauce)

1.25 kg (2½ lb) piece beef fillet
olive oil
freshly ground pepper
30 g (1 oz) butter
¼ cup brandy
béarnaise sauce (see page 113)

Serves: 4
Cooking time: 25 minutes
Oven temperature: 230°C (450°F)

Remove any gristle from the fillet and tie at 2.5 cm (1 in) intervals with string. Brush with olive oil and sprinkle well with freshly ground pepper, leave at room temperature for 1 hour.

Heat 1 tablespoon olive oil in a baking dish with the butter. When sizzling, retain over a brisk heat and add the fillet, turning and browning all over, about 3 minutes.

Heat the brandy, set alight and pour over the fillet. Shake the pan until the flames subside and place in a preheated, very hot oven. Bake for 25 minutes and remove immediately.

Serve cut into thick slices and spoon over the pan juices, hand the bearnaise sauce separately.

Daube de boeuf Provençale

(Stewed beef provençale style)

Any piece of stewing steak can be used in this dish but I find gravy beef has a good flavour and stays succulent.

750 g (1½ lb) piece gravy beef
2 cloves garlic, finely chopped
3 tablespoons olive oil
1½ cups red wine
bouquet garni (comprising large
**   sprig thyme, bay leaf, parsley stalks)**
125 g (4 oz) salt pork
1 large onion, finely chopped
2 carrots, sliced
2 tomatoes, peeled and quartered
½ cup beef stock
1 strip orange peel
salt and freshly ground pepper
freshly chopped parsley

Serves: 4

Cut the beef into large cubes. Combine the garlic, 2 tablespoons olive oil, the wine and the bouquet garni in a large bowl and marinate the beef in this mixture for at least 3 hours. Cut the salt pork into small cubes. Heat remaining oil in a heavy casserole and sauté pork until fat is transparent, about 5 minutes.

Drain the beef, pouring the marinade into a saucepan. Boil rapidly until reduced by half. Add the beef to the salt pork and cook until coloured over a brisk heat. Add the onions and carrots and cook for a further 5 minutes. When marinade has reduced add to the pan with the bouquet garni.

Add the tomatoes, stock and orange peel and season with the salt and freshly ground pepper. Cover and simmer gently for 2-2½ hours or until meat is very tender.

Spoon the meat into a deep serving dish.

Remove the bouquet garni from the sauce and skim the excess fat. Pour over the meat and sprinkle with the parsley. Serve with boiled and buttered noodles and perhaps a crisp green salad.

For a thicker gravy combine 30 g (1 oz) butter with 1½ tablespoons plain flour, whisk into sauce, bring to the boil and simmer a few minutes.

Note: Take care when first seasoning the daube, it reduces considerably and may become too salty. This dish does well if made the day before, allowing the fat to set on the top and be lifted away before reheating.

Navarin of mutton

**750 g (1½ lb) neck of mutton
(preferably from the middle)
salt and freshly ground pepper
2 tablespoons olive oil
1 tablespoon plain flour
2½ cups brown stock
1 clove garlic crushed with a little salt
1 teaspoon tomato paste
bouquet garni (comprising parsley
stalks, sprig of thyme, bay leaf,
a few peppercorns)
8 tiny onions
2 carrots
1 turnip
1 teaspoon sugar**

Serves: 4

Cut the mutton into large cubes and season with the salt and pepper. Heat 1 tablespoon of the oil in a heavy casserole and brown the meat, a few pieces at a time. Sprinkle with the flour, blending well and turning the pieces of meat to coat with the roux. Cook until the flour is browned without burning. Add boiling stock, garlic, tomato paste and bouquet garni. Cover and simmer gently for 45 minutes.

Meanwhile peel the onions, scrape the carrots and cut into large julienne strips about 5 cm x 1 cm (2 in x ½ in). Peel the turnip and cut into the same size strips. In a frying pan heat remaining oil and add sugar and the vegetables. Sauté until the vegetables are a good golden colour.

Lift the meat from the casserole on to a plate. Strain the gravy into a bowl and skim as much fat as possible.

Return the meat to the casserole with the gravy and vegetables. Cover and simmer for a further hour. Pile meat and vegetables into a deep serving dish. Bring the gravy to a boil in a saucepan, skim the fats that come to the surface and spoon over the lamb.

Serve hot with a purée of potatoes.

Gigot d'agneau au vin blanc
(Leg of lamb in white wine)

1 small leg of lamb
salt and pepper
2 cloves garlic
4 medium onions
30 g (1 oz) butter
½ cup dry white wine
bouquet garni (parsley stalks, thyme,
   bay leaf)

Sauce:
125 g (4 oz) butter
1 tablespoon flour
light veal stock or vegetable water
3 egg yolks
1 tablespoon cream
1 tablespoon chopped parsley

Serves: 6
Cooking time: 1¼ hours
Oven temperature: 175°C (350°F)

Wipe the lamb and rub with salt and pepper. Peel garlic and cut into small pieces. Make incisions between the skin and flesh and insert the garlic. Slice onions finely and cook in the baking dish with the butter until soft. Place the meat on the onions and add the wine with 1 cup water. Add the bouquet garni and cover with foil or lid to fit the dish. Bake in a preheated moderate oven until tender, about 1¼ hours.

Place the meat on a heated serving plate and keep warm. Strain liquid from dish and measure. Make up to 2 cups with the addition of a light stock or vegetable water.

Melt 30 g (1 oz) butter in a pan, blend in the flour and cook until a pale straw colour. Add the stock, blending well. Remove from heat and beat in the egg yolks. Whisk until it almost comes to the boil and is thickened. Draw aside and gradually add the butter cut into small pieces, whisking well. Remove from heat, stir in the cream and parsley. Check for seasoning with salt and pepper. Spoon a little over the lamb and serve the rest separately.

Serve with vichy carrots (see page 101) and buttered green beans.

Gigot d'agneau à la Bretonne

(Leg of lamb with haricot beans)

(See photograph opposite)

When the French roast a leg of lamb in the home it is nearly always served with a bowl of haricot beans.

2 kg (4 lb) leg of lamb
salt and freshly ground pepper
1 large clove garlic
1 cup water
30 g (1 oz) butter

Serves: 6
Cooking time: 1¼ hours
Oven temperature: 190°C (375°F)

Wipe lamb and season. Cut a few small incisions between the skin and flesh. Shred garlic and insert into these. Place in a baking dish, preferably on a rack. Put the water, butter and large pinch salt in the dish. Bake in a preheated moderately hot oven for 1¼ hours, basting every 15 minutes. The flesh should be still quite pink.

Serve haricot beans separately.

Gigot d'agneau à la bretonne (Leg of lamb with haricot beans).

Carré d'agneau persillé

(Roast lamb with parsley)

1 kg (2 lb) rack of lamb
salt (4 small rocks) and pepper
½ cup water
¾ cup soft breadcrumbs
1 clove garlic, crushed
½ cup finely chopped parsley
60 g (2 oz) butter, melted

Serves: 4
Cooking time: 40 minutes.
Oven temperature: 200°C (400°F)

Rub racks with salt and pepper and place in a baking dish, fat side up. Pour water into dish and bake in preheated hot oven for 20 minutes, basting occasionally.

Meanwhile combine breadcrumbs, garlic, parsley and melted butter, moistening slightly with drippings from the roasting pan.

Press the mixture thickly over the fat surface of the racks and bake for a further 20 minutes or until the crumbs are golden. Remove meat to heated serving dish. Serve with buttered green beans.

Braised duckling with celery and potato julienne (see recipe on page 78).

Haricot au jus

(Haricot beans)

500 g (1 lb) dried haricot beans
2 large onions, quartered
bouquet garni (parsley stalks, thyme,
   bay leaf)
1 clove garlic
1 teaspoon salt
a few peppercorns
30 g (1 oz) butter
4 shallots, chopped
2 tablespoons chopped parsley

Soak the beans overnight in water to cover, drain. Place in a large saucepan with fresh water to cover, onions, bouquet garni, garlic, salt and peppercorns. Slowly bring to the boil, skim and cover. Cook gently for 1½-2 hours or until tender.

Meanwhile put leg of lamb on to cook. Melt butter in a pan 30 minutes before lamb is due to finish cooking. Add shallots and cook gently until softened, about 2 minutes.

Drain the cooked beans and add to pan, shaking to toss them with the butter and shallots. Add ½ cup of the lamb juices from the dish. Cover and simmer gently for a further 15 minutes.

Place the lamb on a serving platter and strain the juices from the dish into a sauceboat. Toss the beans with parsley and serve separately.

Note: 1 tomato, peeled and roughly chopped, can be added to the shallots before adding the cooked beans.

Tournedos morateur
(Fillet steaks with anchovy butter sauce)

The strong and salty flavour of canned anchovies combines well with beef.
An idea when roasting beef, instead of rubbing salt on the fat, is to arrange a
lattice of anchovy fillets over the meat and leave to marinate for a few hours
before roasting at a high temperature.

4 x 4 cm (1½ in) fillet steaks　　　　　　　　　　　　　　Serves: 4
45 g (1½ oz) butter
3 anchovy fillets, finely chopped
freshly ground pepper
1 shallot, finely chopped
½ cup dry white wine

Trim the steaks of any gristle or fat and pull into neat round shapes by tying
with string.

Soften 30 g (1 oz) of the butter in a small bowl using a wooden spoon. Add
the anchovy fillets and pound well to a smooth paste. Season with freshly
ground pepper.

Heat remaining butter in a frying pan and when sizzling hot add the steaks,
cook over a brisk heat for 3 minutes on one side, turn and cook for a further 3
minutes. Place on a serving plate and keep warm. Add the shallots to the pan,
cook gently for about 3 minutes.

Pour on the wine and reduce by half. Stir in the anchovy butter and simmer for
a few minutes. Pour over the steaks and serve immediately.

Escalopes de veau sautées

Ask the butcher to cut 1 cm (½ in) slices of escalopes from the thick end of the leg and then flatten them out for you. This is a simple dish and delicious if the veal is good. When choosing veal be sure that it is pearly pink with white fat.

4 veal escalopes
seasoned plain flour
30 g (1 oz) butter
½ cup dry white wine or light
   veal stock
finely chopped parsley

Serves: 4

Dust the veal with the seasoned flour. Melt the butter in a large frying pan and sauté the veal escalopes on a medium heat until golden on both sides and tender, about 6 minutes. Place on a heated serving dish.

Add the white wine or stock to the pan, stirring well and bring to a rapid boil. Allow to reduce by half then pour over the veal. Sprinkle with the parsley and serve.

Côtes de veau à la crème

(Veal chops with cream sauce)

2 tablespoons oil or butter
4 veal chops
salt and pepper
2 tablespoons dry sherry
½ cup finely chopped parsley
⅔ cup cream

Serves: 4

Heat oil in frying pan and brown chops lightly on both sides. Season with salt and pepper and continue to cook over gentle heat for 20 minutes, turning them occasionally. When cooked remove to heated platter.

Pour sherry into frying pan and scrape the crusting dripping from the pan. Add the chopped parsley and cream. Heat but do not allow to boil. Season to taste with salt and pepper and spoon sauce over chops.

Serve immediately with buttered noodles or rice.

Herb-buttered noodles

250 g (½ lb) noodles
1 clove garlic (optional)
60 g (2 oz) butter
1 tablespoon chopped parsley
1 tablespoon chopped basil
freshly ground pepper

Serves: 4

Bring 2.25 litres (4 pints) of salted water to boil. Add noodles and boil briskly stirring occasionally for 15-20 minutes or until the noodles are just tender.

Crush garlic and beat into butter with parsley and basil. Drain noodles in colander and place in heated serving dish. Add herbed butter and toss noodles lightly till well coated. Sprinkle with pepper and extra herbs if wished and serve immediately.

Blanquette de veau

This is a classic recipe which is superbly simple. The name refers to the blanket of cream sauce coating the veal.

1 kg (2 lb) shoulder veal
1 carrot
1 onion
1 celery stalk
90 g (3 oz) butter
2½ cups boiling water
1 veal bone
bouquet garni (comprising parsley
   stalks, sprig of thyme, bay leaf,
   a few peppercorns)
pinch salt
1½ tablespoons plain flour
2 egg yolks
⅔ cup cream
¼ cup lemon juice
salt and white pepper

Serves: 4-6

Cut the veal into large cubes 5 cm x 5 cm (2 in x 2 in). Scrape and slice the carrots, quarter the onion and cut celery into thick slices. In a casserole melt 30 g (1 oz) butter over a gentle heat. Add the vegetables and sauté until softened, about 5 minutes. Add the veal, tossing well in the butter and cook a further 5 minutes, without colouring. Pour on the boiling water and add the veal bone, bouquet garni and pinch salt. Cover and simmer gently for 1½ hours or until veal is tender.

Melt remaining butter in a small pan. Blend in the flour and stir in 1½ cups veal liquid. Bring to the boil, stirring constantly and simmer for 5 minutes.

Beat the egg yolks with the cream and lemon juice. Add a little of the hot sauce and pour the liaison back into the pan. Season to taste with salt and pepper and allow the sauce to reheat without boiling.

Lift the meat from the liquid and vegetables and place in a serving casserole. Pour over the sauce and serve with boiled rice tossed in parsley.

Cervelles au beurre noir

(Brains with black butter)

750 g (1½ lb) brains
1 tablespoon vinegar
1 teaspoon salt
few peppercorns
1 clove garlic
bouquet garni (comprising parsley
    stalks and a bay leaf)
2½ cups water

Serves: 4

Sauce:
90 g (3 oz) butter
2 tablespoons chopped parsley
2 teaspoons vinegar

Soak the brains in water to cover for 2 hours, changing the water frequently. Drain and remove the skin with any loose fibres. In a wide shallow pan combine the vinegar, salt, peppercorns, peeled garlic clove and bouquet garni with the water. Bring slowly to the boil, reduce heat and add brains. Poach gently for 15 minutes. Drain and arrange on a heated serving plate. Keep warm.

Make the sauce by melting the butter and cooking until a light brown. Add the chopped parsley and fry gently for 3 minutes. Spoon over brains and return pan to heat. Add vinegar and bring to the boil. Pour over brains and serve immediately.

Longe de porc boulangère

(Loin of pork with potatoes)

**2 kg (4 lb) loin of pork boned and
  with the skin removed**
salt and freshly ground pepper
1 small garlic clove, finely chopped
8 medium potatoes
1 onion, chopped
15 g (½ oz) butter
1½ cups dry white wine
¾ cup water

Serves: 6
Cooking time: 2½ hours
Oven temperature: 180ºC (350ºF)

Season the inside of the loin of pork with the salt, freshly ground pepper and garlic. Roll and tie at 2.5 cm (1 in) intervals.

Place on a baking dish and bake in a preheated moderate oven for 1 hour. Slice the potatoes and add to the pan with the onions, butter, white wine, water, salt and freshly ground pepper. Return to the oven and cook a further 1½ hours or until the pork juices run clear when tested with a fine skewer. The liquid should be almost absorbed and the potatoes tender and golden.

Place the pork on a large heated platter and spoon the potatoes around.

Note: Unlike the English, who like their roast pork to have a crisp golden crackling, the French remove it when roasting and use the rind to give extra flavour to their braises.

Côtes de porc Normande

(Pork chops with cider)

4 thick pork loin chops
75 g (1½ oz) butter
30 g (1 oz) grated Parmesan cheese
¼ cup cream
⅓ cup cider
1 teaspoon wine vinegar
⅓ cup white stock or vegetable water
1 teaspoon French mustard
salt and freshly ground pepper
2 cooking apples

Serves: 4
Cooking time: 15-20 minutes
Oven temperature: 175°C (350°F)

Trim the pork chops of skin and excess fat. Melt 30 g (1 oz) butter in a frying pan and sauté the pork until golden on both sides, about 5 minutes. Combine the cheese with 1 tablespoon of the cream and spread over the chops.

Lay them in a small baking dish. Bake in a preheated moderate oven for 20 minutes until tender. Arrange the chops on a heated serving dish and keep warm.

Add the cider and vinegar to the baking dish, boil until reduced to a glaze. Add the stock, cream and seasonings and simmer gently for 2 minutes. Spoon over the chops.

Meanwhile peel and slice apples thickly. Heat remaining butter in a small frying pan and fry the apple rings until golden. Arrange around the pork chops.

Serve hot with boiled potatoes tossed in melted butter and chopped parsley.

Tripes vinaigrette

1 kg (2 lb) tripe
water
¾ cup vinaigrette dressing (see
  page 117)
2 tablespoons chopped parsley

Serves: 4

Boil the tripe as in Tripes Lyonnaises (see page 66) for 1½ hours. Cut into strips and while still warm, toss in vinaigrette dressing and half the parsley.

Pile into a serving bowl and allow to cool. Sprinkle with remaining parsley and serve chilled with crusty bread.

Note: Tripe is also good with aïoli. Toss prepared tripe in ½ cup vinaigrette, ¼ cup aïoli and parsley. Serve sprinkled with remaining parsley.

Tripes Lyonnaises

(Tripe Lyons style)

When the name Lyonnais applies to a dish it usually means with onions. This dish, with its own wine and butter sauce, differs greatly from the English style tripe and onions with parsley sauce.

1 kg (2 lb) tripe
1 teaspoon salt
60 g (2 oz) butter
4 large onions, finely sliced
1 clove garlic, finely chopped
salt and freshly ground pepper
1½ cups dry white wine
2 tablespoons lemon juice
1 tablespoon chopped parsley

Serves: 4

Leaving the tripe in a piece, place in a large pan and cover with water. Bring to the boil and drain off liquid. Add fresh water to just cover and salt, bring to the boil, cover and simmer gently until tender, about 1 hour. Drain and cut into thin 5 cm (2 in) strips.

Heat half the butter in a frying pan and sauté the onions and garlic until golden. Add remaining butter with tripe and cook a further 5 minutes. Season with salt and pepper and pour on the wine. Cook briskly for 1 minute. Reduce heat, cover and simmer gently for 30 minutes. Add lemon juice and transfer to a heated serving dish.

Sprinkle with the parsley and serve hot with new potatoes.

Poultry and rabbit

How clever of the French to have discovered that poultry can be cooked in so many delicious and different ways, and not just confined to the roasting pan.

One of the nicest ways of cooking chicken is the simple method of sautéeing. The chicken is first cut, with the aid of a sharp knife and pair of poultry scissors, into neat serving pieces. Then each piece is cooked briskly in butter or oil until it is almost cooked. The ingredients that give each sauté dish its name are added and cooked just long enough for the flavours to develop.

The French roast chicken in a special way that keeps the bird moist and plump while making its own sauce. Sometimes the chicken is stuffed but more often a bouquet of fresh herbs, a grinding of fresh pepper and a knob of butter is all that is necessary.

Duck is superb both roasted and braised. It is nearly always cooked these ways but has many traditional garnishes which provide a great deal of variety. These garnishes also help to balance the richness of duck.

They are equally imaginative when it comes to rabbit. It is usually casseroled, often with bacon or tomatoes, in a wonderful array of sauces. The mustard of Dijon is used to great advantage in the well-known dish Lapin au Moutarde.

French roast chicken

Chicken, roasted in the French manner with a little liquid added to the pan, has an ensured moistness. Without becoming stewed, the steam that rises is just enough to stop the bird drying out.

1.5 kg (3 lb) chicken
60 g (2 oz) butter
salt, freshly ground pepper
large pinch dried tarragon or few
    parsley stalks
strip orange or lemon rind
¼ cup white wine

Serves: 4
Cooking time: 1 hour
Oven temperature: 190°C (375°F)
lower to: 180°C (350°F)

Wipe the cavity of the chicken with a damp cloth. Place half the butter inside with seasonings, herbs and rind. Truss, folding the wing tips under the bird and running the string from the back end over the wings, crossing underneath and then tying the two drumsticks together.

Wipe outside of bird and spread with remaining butter. Place in a small baking dish, preferably on a rack. Pour ½ cup water in the pan with the wine and place in a preheated moderately hot oven for 15 minutes. After this time turn the bird on its side and lower oven temperature to moderate. Cook for a further 15 minutes and turn to the other side. Baste the chicken frequently with the pan juices and turn the bird with the breast up for the last 10 minutes, to become golden.

To test if the bird is done, run a fine skewer into the thickest part of the thigh. The juices should run clear without any pink tinge.

Place the chicken on a heated serving dish and remove trussing strings. Bring the pan juices to a rapid boil and cook for a few minutes to amalgamate. Season with salt and pepper and spoon a little over the chicken. Serve the rest separately.

Poule-au-pot

(Chicken in a pot)

A boiling fowl is best for this well-known dish. It is stuffed with fresh pork and herbs then poached until tender in plenty of liquid and vegetables.

1 boiling fowl, or 1 x 1.75 kg
   (3½ lb) chicken
250 g (8 oz) pork shoulder,
   finely chopped
2 tablespoons chopped mixed herbs
1 egg
salt and freshly ground pepper
15 g (½ oz) butter
1 onion, celery stalk and carrot, sliced
2 cups boiling water
bouquet garni (comprising parsley
   stalks, sprig thyme, bay leaf)

Serves: 6

Sauce:
15 g (1 oz) butter
1 tablespoon plain flour
1 cup hot cooking liquid
2 egg yolks
1 cup cream
salt, freshly ground white pepper

Remove the giblets from chicken and wipe cavity.

In a bowl combine the pork, herbs, egg and seasonings. Stuff chicken with pork mixture and tie legs together with string. In a large casserole melt the butter. When foaming add the chicken and brown all over turning frequently, about every 10 minutes. Remove and keep warm.

Add the sliced vegetables to the pan and sauté until softened and golden. Place chicken on top and pour on the boiling water. Add bouquet garni, salt and pepper. Slowly bring to the boil, cover and reduce heat to a simmer. Cook gently for about 2½ hours.

Place the chicken in a serving casserole and strain off the liquid into a bowl. Discard the vegetables and skim the fat from the liquid. Reserve 1 cup of liquid for the sauce and store remaining as stock. Keep the chicken warm while making sauce.

Melt the butter in a pan, blend in the flour and cook until a pale straw colour.

Gradually add the liquid, stirring constantly until it comes to the boil. Beat the egg yolks with the cream in a small bowl and pour on a little of the hot sauce. Combine and pour this liaison back into the pan of hot sauce. Heat gently for a few minutes until thickened slightly. Check seasoning with salt and pepper, spoon a little over the chicken and pour the rest into a sauceboat.

Serve the chicken surrounded with freshly boiled vegetables. Hand around the sauce separately.

Poulet Normande
(Chicken with apples)

Normandy is famous for butter, fresh cream and eggs. It has excellent poultry, its rivers are filled with fish and while it does not have its own wine, its magnificent orchards are filled with little apples which produce the superb apple brandy called Calvados, and naturally, cider. Our own chickens respond well to this recipe from Normandy, the combination of chicken and apples being most agreeable.

1.75 kg (3½ lb) chicken   Serves: 4
30 g (1 oz) butter
1 tablespoon oil
1 large onion, finely chopped
1 tablespoon plain flour
3 tablespoons Calvados or brandy
1½ cups apple cider
bouquet garni
salt and freshly ground pepper
2 cooking apples
¼ cup cream

Cut the chicken into neat serving pieces. Melt butter with oil in a heavy sauté pan and cook the chicken on both sides until golden, about 10 minutes. Add the onion to the pan and cook a further few minutes. Blend in the flour and cook until a pale straw colour.

Heat the Calvados or brandy, set alight and pour over the chicken, cook briskly until flames subside, shaking the pan all the time then pour in the cider. Add the bouquet garni, season with salt and freshly ground pepper, cover and simmer gently for 20 minutes or until tender.

Arrange chicken on serving dish and keep warm.

Peel and dice the apples, add to the pan and cook briskly until soft, about 3 minutes. Stir in cream, reheat and check for seasoning. Spoon the sauce over chicken and serve.

Poulet sauté ronsard

Many French restaurants win world acclaim for the excellence of cooking local dishes. This recipe comes from a small restaurant, Le Cheval Rouge in Montoire. Its owner has won many awards for this fine cooking and this chicken dish is one of his specialities.

1.5 kg (3 lb) chicken
seasoned plain flour
4 tablespoons olive oil
3 carrots, finely chopped
½ cup finely chopped shallots
1 clove garlic, crushed
½ cup brandy
1 cup dry white wine
1 tomato, peeled, seeded
   and chopped
bouquet garni (comprising parsley
   stalks, sprig thyme, bay leaf)
1 cup cream
freshly chopped parsley

Serves: 4

Cut the chicken into serving pieces. Dust with the seasoned flour. Heat the olive oil in a frying pan and sauté the chicken on both sides until golden. Add the carrots, shallots, and garlic and cook for a further few minutes.

Heat the brandy and flame over the chicken. Add the wine, tomato and bouquet garni, cover and simmer gently for 30 minutes or until tender. Arrange the chicken pieces on a heated serving dish and keep warm.

Add the cream to the pan and boil briskly for a few minutes, season with salt and pepper. Strain through a sieve pressing the vegetables well and pour the sauce over the chicken. Sprinkle with the chopped parsley and serve with saffron rice.

Saffron rice: Heat 3 tablespoons olive oil in a heavy pan and cook 1 onion, finely chopped, until soft without colouring. Add 1 cup long grain rice and stir well to coat the rice with the oil.

Cook for 1 minute and add 2 cups hot water and a large pinch saffron soaked in 2 tablespoons warm water. Season with a pinch salt. Add a knob of butter. Cover and simmer gently for about 15 minutes or until rice is tender.

Pile into a round casserole and serve separately with the Chicken ronsard.

Poulet sauté à l'estragon

(Chicken sauté with tarragon)
(See photograph opposite)

Although chicken responds well to many herbs and seasonings, it shares a rare affinity with tarragon. Unfortunately, the true tarragon can only be grown in France and even though it may grow here it soon reverts into a herb, slightly bitter and the flavour not even comparable to the true French variety. If possible use dried tarragon, imported from France, and leave the fresh tarragon for garnishing.

1.75 kg (3½ lb) chicken   Serves: 4
60 g (2 oz) butter
2 shallots, finely chopped
1 tablespoon plain flour
¾ cup dry white wine
½ cup chicken stock
2 teaspoons dried tarragon
salt and freshly ground pepper
squeeze lemon juice
1 tablespoon cream
fresh tarragon to garnish (optional)

Cut the chicken into neat serving pieces and wipe with a kitchen towel. Melt the butter in a sauté pan and add the chicken pieces, skin side down first. Sauté until golden on both sides. Reduce heat, cover and continue cooking until tender, about 20 minutes. Arrange chicken on a heated serving dish and keep warm.

Add the shallots to the pan and cook until softened, about 1 minute. Blend in the flour and cook until a pale straw colour. Stir in the wine and reduce by half. Add the stock, tarragon and seasonings, blend well and simmer gently for 5 minutes. Season with lemon juice and strain through a sieve into a small pan. Add the cream and spoon a little over the chicken. Serve the rest separately with the chicken which may be garnished with the tarragon.

Poulet sauté à l'estragon (Chicken sauté with tarragon).

Poulet à l'ail

(Chicken with garlic)
(See photograph opposite)

1.75 kg (3½ lb) chicken
salt and freshly ground pepper
½ cup olive oil
10 garlic cloves, peeled
bouquet garni (comprising thyme,
**   sage, rosemary, parsley, bay leaf)**

Serves: 4
Cooking time: 1 hour
Oven temperature: 180°C (350°F)

Wipe the chicken and season with salt and freshly ground pepper, including the cavity. Truss into a neat shape with string. Heat the olive oil in a deep casserole and add chicken turning until golden all over. Add the garlic cloves and bouquet garni, cover and bake in a preheated moderate oven for 1 hour.

Discard garlic and herbs and serve the chicken with a crisp salad and slices of crusty French bread.

Poulet à l'ail (Chicken with garlic).

Poulet sauté chasseur

(Chicken sauteed hunter style)

1.75 kg (3½ lb) chicken
2 tablespoons olive oil
30 g (1 oz) butter
2 tablespoons brandy
½ cup dry white wine
1 cup chicken stock
salt and freshly ground pepper
2 tablespoons chopped herbs
2 tablespoons tomato paste
parsley

Serves: 4

Cut the chicken into serving pieces and wipe with a kitchen towel. In a large frying pan or sauté pan heat oil and melt butter. When the butter is foaming add the chicken. Sauté them on both sides until golden. Heat the brandy, set alight and pour over the chicken. Shake the pan until the flames subside.

Add the wine and reduce the liquid by half. Add stock, seasonings and herbs with tomato paste. Cover the pan and cook gently for about 20 minutes.

Sprinkle with freshly chopped parsley and serve with sautéed potatoes.

Coq au vin
(Chicken cooked with red wine)

Coq au Vin was devised in the days when an older, mature bird was often used, and long slow cooking was required, giving a rich full flavour so well known and loved. Younger chickens suitable for roasting or sautéeing are more common now and so I have adapted the recipe to suit. The rich red wine sauce is cooked first and then added to the chicken just long enough for it to become tender and to allow the fine flavour of the sauce to impregnate the chicken.

30 g (1 oz) butter
1 large onion, finely chopped
2 cloves garlic, crushed
1½ tablespoons plain flour
3 cups dry red wine, preferably
   burgundy
bouquet garni (comprising parsley
   stalks, large sprig thyme, bay leaf)
salt and freshly ground pepper
1.75 kg (3½ lb) chicken
60 g (2 oz) salt pork
12 tiny onions
12 button mushrooms
½ cup brandy
freshly chopped parsley

Serves: 4-6
Cooking time: 1½ hours

Melt half the butter in a saucepan. Add the onion and garlic and cook until transparent, about 5 minutes. Stir in the flour and blend in the wine. Continue stirring and bring to the boil. Add bouquet garni, salt and freshly ground pepper, cover and simmer gently for 1 hour.

Cut the chicken into serving pieces and wipe dry. Heat remaining butter in a casserole and sauté the chicken on both sides until light golden. Set aside and keep warm.

Cut the salt pork into small cubes. Peel the onions, wipe the mushrooms and trim the stalks. Add to the pan and sauté briskly for a few minutes until golden.

Return the chicken to the pan. Warm the brandy, set alight and pour over the chicken. Cook briskly for 1 minute, shaking the pan and when the flames subside add the wine sauce. Cover and simmer gently for 30 minutes or until chicken is tender. Serve sprinkled with chopped parsley.

Braised duckling with celery and potato julienne

(See photograph on page 56)

In France duckling has many traditional garnishes, all of which seem to blend perfectly with the wonderfully rich flavour. Prepare Braised Duckling as on opposite page and surround with the following garnish:

**1 head celery
3 medium potatoes
2 shallots
30 g (1 oz) butter
salt and freshly ground pepper
1 tablespoon chopped parsley**

Remove tough outer stalks of celery. Cut remaining into julienne strips, about 5 cm x .3 cm (2 in x ⅛ in). Peel potatoes and cut into strips the same size. Chop shallots finely.

Melt butter in a pan and sauté celery and shallots until softened, without colouring. Add potatoes and seasonings, cover with a piece of buttered greaseproof paper and cook gently for about 15 minutes, or until tender.

Toss with parsley and arrange around duckling.

Braised duckling

2 kg (4 lb) duckling
30 g (1 oz) butter
1 carrot, chopped
1 onion, chopped
1 small turnip, chopped (optional)
1 small celery stalk, chopped
1 cup dry white wine
bouquet garni (comprising parsley
**   stalks, sprig of thyme, bay leaf,**
**   a few peppercorns)**
salt and freshly ground pepper
1 teaspoon arrowroot or cornflour
2 teaspoons port

Serves: 4
Cooking time: 1½ hours
Oven temperature: 190°C (375°F)

Wipe the duckling with a cloth and truss with string into a neat shape. Melt the butter in a heavy casserole and brown duckling all over. Set aside and keep warm. Add the chopped vegetables to the pan and sauté until softened and light golden. Pour off fat from pan and place duckling on vegetables. Add the wine, bouquet garni, salt and pepper. Cover and bake in a preheated moderately hot oven for 1½ hours, cook the duck on both sides, placing the breast up for last 15 minutes. Put the duck on a heated serving dish and keep warm.

Skim the fat from the pan and place on a direct heat. Mix the arrowroot with the port and stir in a little of the hot liquid. Pour into the pan juices and bring to the boil, stirring constantly. Remove from heat immediately and check for seasoning with salt and freshly ground pepper.

Spoon a little over the duck and strain the rest into a sauceboat. Serve with buttered peas.

Braised duckling with glazed turnips

This dish should be made when the small and very young white turnips are in season. Turnips, called **navets** in France, are one of the most popular garnishes for duckling. Prepare Braised Duckling (see page 79) and garnish with the following:

1 kg (2 lb) white turnips
pinch salt
2 teaspoons sugar
60 g (2 oz) butter
1 cup water

Peel and quarter the turnips, or if they are large cut into eights. If a little older than desired place in a saucepan and cover with cold water, bring to the boil and cook for 3-4 minutes, drain and return to saucepan. Now add remaining ingredients. Cover and cook until just tender, about 10 minutes.

Remove cover and boil rapidly, allowing the liquid to evaporate completely, leaving a thick syrup to glaze the turnips. Be careful at this stage not to burn the sugar and butter.

Set the Braised Duckling on a dish and arrange the glazed turnips around. Finish as in basic recipe.

Canard aux cerises

(Duckling with cherries)

Roast duckling is often served with fruit which helps to counteract the rich flavour and extreme fattiness of the bird. Cherries, peaches, orange and pineapple could all be used, they require only to be glazed or heated either in butter or port then served with the duckling.

2 kg (4 lb) duckling
few celery leaves (optional)
strip lemon peel
salt and freshly ground pepper
1 clove garlic
1 cup white wine
400 g (14 oz) jar sour cherries
¼ cup port wine
1 teaspoon arrowroot

Serves: 4
Cooking time: 1¼ hours
Oven temperature: 200°C (400°F)
lower to: 180°C (350°F)

Remove neck and giblets from duckling and gently simmer in 1½ cups water for 1 hour to make stock.

Wipe duckling and stuff with celery leaves and lemon peel. Season the outside with salt and pepper. Crack the clove of garlic with the flat of a knife and rub over skin. Truss with string into a neat shape and place on a rack in a baking dish. Bake in a preheated hot oven for 15 minutes.

Pour off fat from dish and add white wine. Cover breast with a piece of foil or brown paper and return to a moderate oven for a further 1 hour.

Place duck on a heated serving plate, remove trussing string and return to oven which has been turned off.

Skim fat from juices in dish and place on a direct heat. Pour in strained duck stock and boil rapidly until reduced by half.

Drain the cherries and place in a saucepan. Add the port and heat gently. Strain the port into the sauce and spoon the cherries around the duck. Continue boiling the sauce for 2 minutes. Combine the arrowroot with 2 teaspoons water, add a little of the hot sauce and pour back into pan. Bring to the boil and remove immediately. Check for seasoning with salt and pepper.

Spoon a little of the sauce over the duck and serve the rest separately. To serve the duck, cut in half and cut again into 4 pieces.

Lapin moutarde

(Rabbit with mustard)

1 rabbit
2 teaspoons vinegar
pinch salt
seasoned plain flour
6 small onions
1 tablespoon olive oil
30 g (1 oz) butter
125 g (4 oz) streaky bacon, in the piece
3 cups light chicken stock
salt and freshly ground pepper
2 tablespoons French mustard
bouquet garni (comprising parsley
   stalks, sprig of thyme, bay leaf, a
   few peppercorns)
½ cup cream
1 tablespoon freshly chopped parsley

Serves: 4
Cooking time: 1½ hours

Cut the rabbit into serving pieces and soak overnight in vinegar, pinch salt and water to cover. Drain and dry with a kitchen towel. Dust with the seasoned flour.

Peel and quarter the onions, heat the oil and melt the butter in a heavy casserole, add the onions and cook for 3 minutes until light golden, remove and keep warm.

Add the rabbit and the diced bacon and sauté until golden. Pour in stock with seasonings, mustard and bouquet garni. Return onions, cover and simmer gently for 1½ hours or until tender. Arrange the rabbit on a heated serving dish.

Boil the sauce briskly until reduced by half and add cream. Bring to the boil, check for seasonings and adjust with salt and freshly ground pepper. Pour over the rabbit and sprinkle with parsley.

Fish and shellfish

With its enormous coastline and freeflowing rivers, France has a huge variety of fish – and there is no snobbery. From the abundant mackerel to the expensive sole, each has its own merit. We also have a huge selection and although the fish differ slightly they adapt admirably to the French style of cooking.

Filets de St Pierre Normande
(Fillets of John Dory with prawns)

The name Normande often means that a dish has plenty of cream and eggs or is cooked with cider and apples. The coastal waters of Normandy are filled with all kinds of seafood, including shellfish and so the name may also apply to a garnish of prawns, oysters or mussels.

4-6 John Dory fillets
2 cups water
1 cup dry white wine
bouquet garni (comprising bay leaf, parsley stalks, a few black peppercorns)
1 small onion, sliced
1 celery stalk, sliced
1 teaspoon salt

Serves: 4

Sauce:
60 g (2 oz) butter
2 tablespoons plain flour
1½ cups fish stock
½ cup cream
1 tablespoon lemon juice
salt and white pepper
250 g (8 oz) fresh school prawns, shelled

Remove the skin from the fish fillets. In a pan add the water, white wine, bouquet garni, sliced onion, celery stalk and salt. Slowly bring to the boil and simmer gently for 5 minutes.

Fold the fish fillets in three. Reduce the heat and add the fish to the pan. Cover with a piece of buttered greaseproof paper and poach gently for 8 minutes.

Arrange the fish fillets on a heated serving dish, cover with the piece of greaseproof paper and keep warm while making the sauce.

Melt 45 g (1½ oz) of the butter in a small pan. Blend in the flour and cook until a pale straw colour. Strain the fish cooking liquid, measure 1½ cups and add to the roux, stirring constantly. Bring to the boil and simmer gently for 5 minutes. Add remaining butter, cream, lemon juice, salt and pepper to taste and shelled prawns.

Reheat and coat the fish fillets with the sauce. Serve immediately with fish potatoes (see recipe on page 88).

Petits pains de poisson nantua

(Tiny fish creams with prawn sauce)

A superb entrée for a special dinner party. It involves a fair amount of preparation but most can be done well ahead.

500 g (1 lb) snapper fillets
30 g (1 oz) butter
1 tablespoon plain flour
1 cup milk
1 bay leaf
1 egg
1 egg yolk
salt and pepper

Nantua sauce:
60 g (2 oz) butter
250 g (8 oz) prawns
1½ tablespoons plain flour
1¼ cups fish stock
¼ cup cream
salt and freshly ground pepper

Serves: 4
Cooking time: 20 minutes
Oven temperature: 180°C (350°F)

Lay the fillets on a piece of wet greaseproof paper. With a spoon flake the fish from the skin and bones. Place in a large bowl and pound with the end of a rolling pin or a pestle.

Heat milk with bay leaf and allow to infuse. Melt the butter in a pan and blend in the flour. Add the milk, stir until it boils and simmer a few minutes until thickened, remove bay leaf. Allow to cool.

When cold gradually beat into the fish until a smooth paste. Add the egg and yolk and season to taste with salt and pepper.

Butter 8 small dariole moulds or use a ring mould. Fill with the fish mixture to about .5 cm (¼ in) from the top. Cover each with a round of buttered greaseproof paper or foil and place in a pan of hot water. Bake in a preheated moderate oven for 20 minutes.

To serve, unmould on to a heated serving dish and coat each with the nantua sauce.

To make sauce melt half the butter in a pan and add the unshelled prawns. Simmer gently for 5 minutes.

Purée in a blender or pound well, then rub through a sieve to a thick paste, this could easily be done the day before as it is time consuming.

Melt remaining butter and blend in the flour. Add the stock and stir until boiling. Simmer gently for 5 minutes then add the cream and prawn butter.

Season to taste with salt and freshly ground pepper and spoon over each fish cream.

Poisson au beurre blanc

(Poached snapper with white butter sauce)

1.5 kg (3 lb) snapper
1 onion, sliced
1 carrot, sliced
bay leaf
parsley stalks
a few peppercorns
2 cups water
1 cup dry white wine
¼ cup finely chopped shallots
3 tablespoons fish liquid
185 g (6 oz) butter
¼ cup fresh cream

Serves: 4
Cooking time: 25 minutes
Oven temperature: 160°C (325°F)

Scale and wash the fish and place in a baking dish with the onion, carrot, bay leaf, parsley stalks, peppercorns, water and half the wine. Cover with a piece of buttered greaseproof paper and bake in a preheated moderately slow oven for 25 minutes or until the flesh can be easily lifted from the bone. Keep warm while preparing sauce.

Boil rapidly together the white wine, shallots and fish cooking liquid to about 2 tablespoons. Remove from heat and place over a pan of warm water. Gradually whisk in the butter in small pieces. Whisk until almost frothy, adding the cream gradually.

Place the fish on a heated serving dish and remove the skin. Serve immediately with the sauce separately and steamed fish potatoes (see page 88).

St Pierre meunière

(John Dory with butter and parsley sauce)

4 John Dory fillets
seasoned plain flour
60 g (2 oz) butter
juice ½ lemon
1 tablespoon finely chopped parsley

Serves: 4

Remove the dark skin from the fish fillets. Dry them with a kitchen towel and dust with the seasoned flour.

Heat half the butter in a frying pan, when sizzling add the fish fillets and cook for about 2 minutes on each side until tender and golden. Now add the lemon juice and remaining butter to the pan, cook briskly until amalgamated and add the parsley.

Arrange the fish on a heated serving dish, spoon over the pan juices and serve immediately.

Filets de poisson en papilotte
(Fillets of fish in paper)

This fish is cooked in one large piece of foil but individual servings can be cooked separately. Oven bags or buttered greaseproof paper may substitute for the foil.

4 x 185 g (6 oz) snapper fillets,
  skinned
4 slices lemon
3 tablespoons dry white wine
freshly ground pepper
4 thin bacon rashers, halved
2 tablespoons finely chopped parsley
1 tablespoon olive oil
1 bay leaf, crumbled
2 small garlic cloves, finely chopped
sprig of thyme, finely chopped
pinch chopped savory (optional)

Serves: 4
Cooking time: 20 minutes
Oven temperature: 200°C (400°F)

Sauce:
2 tablespoons finely chopped shallots
4 tablespoons dry white wine
125 g (4 oz) butter
1 tablespoon lemon juice
freshly ground white pepper

Place the fish fillets flat in a dish and put a slice of lemon on each. Sprinkle with the dry white wine and pepper and leave to marinate for 1 hour.

Cut each fillet into 2 neat pieces and wrap half a bacon rasher around each. Arrange on a large piece of foil and sprinkle with the parsley, olive oil, bay leaf and remaining ingredients.

Fold the foil over to enclose the fish and seal the edges. Place on a baking dish and bake in a preheated hot oven for 20 minutes or until tender. Transfer to a serving plate and remove the pieces of bay leaf. Serve the sauce separately.

To make the sauce cook the shallots in a small saucepan with the wine until it has reduced to 1 tablespoon. Remove from the heat and gradually stir in the butter in very small pieces. Continue stirring until it is all added, it should remain yellow and creamy without becoming oily. Stir in the lemon juice and season with freshly ground white pepper.

Maquereaux Algérienne

(Mackerel in tomato and pepper sauce)

4 small mackerel
salt and pepper
squeeze of lemon juice
2 green or red peppers
2 ripe tomatoes
15 g (½ oz) butter or oil
1 small onion, finely chopped
1 clove garlic, crushed

Serves: 4
Cooking time: 10-15 minutes
Oven temperature: 180°C (350°F)

Ask the fishmonger to fillet and skin the mackerel. Place in lightly buttered baking dish. Season with salt and freshly ground pepper and moisten with lemon juice.

Bake in preheated moderate oven 10-15 minutes or until flesh flakes easily.

Meanwhile prepare the sauce. Cut the peppers into thin strips. Cover with boiling water, bring to boil then rinse under cold water. Peel and chop tomatoes.

Melt the butter or oil, fry onion till soft, add tomatoes and garlic. Simmer slowly for 15 minutes. Add the peppers and cook for a further 2-3 minutes. Season to taste with salt and pepper.

Spoon the mixture over the fish and serve garnished with thin slices of lemon and chopped parsley.

Fish potatoes

A classic garnish with poached fish, these potatoes are shaped into small ovals and steamed in a colander over boiling water.

4 medium potatoes
pinch salt
1 tablespoon finely chopped parsley

Peel the potatoes and cut into halves lengthwise. Using a potato peeler pare the sharp edges to shape into ovals. Place in a colander, sprinkle with salt.

Cover with a lid and steam over a pan of boiling water for about 15 minutes. Sprinkle with parsley and serve.

Skate with black butter sauce

Skate, the 'wings' of stingrays, has a delicious flavour, the flesh is thick and creamy and most digestible. Served with Black Butter Sauce it is one of the classic dishes of French cooking. It is not difficult to do but does require last minute attention.

1 wing of skate weighing 750 g-1 kg   Serves: 4
  (1½-2 lb)
water to cover
3 teaspoons salt
1 tablespoon vinegar
1 bay leaf
1 onion, sliced
4 peppercorns
few parsley stalks

Black butter sauce:
3 teaspoons chopped capers
60 g (2 oz) butter, preferably unsalted
2 tablespoons wine vinegar

Wash the skate and cut into serving pieces. Place in wide pan. Cover with cold water, add the seasonings and bring to the boil. Simmer very gently for 20-25 minutes depending how thick the pieces are.

Lift with a fish slice on to a board or clean folded tea towel. Scrape away the skin from both sides and lift flesh from the large cartilaginous bone. Transfer to a heated serving dish, sprinkle with chopped parsley and keep hot while making the black butter sauce.

Sprinkle chopped capers over fish. Heat a small frying pan, drop in the butter and heat carefully till it turns brown but not in the least burnt. Pour quickly over fish.

Add the vinegar to pan and reduce to half, this only takes a second. Pour over fish and serve immediately.

St Pierre aïoli
(John Dory with garlic mayonnaise)

Poach John Dory fillets (as in recipe page 84) in water, wine and bouquet garni. Allow to cool in liquid. Drain fish and arrange on a serving platter.

Beat 1 cup of aïoli (see page 116) with enough of the fish cooking liquid to give a smooth coating consistency. Spoon over fish and sprinkle with finely chopped parsley.

Note: This dish can be chilled but is really more delicious made a few hours before serving.

Coquilles à la Parisienne

(Scallops with mushrooms)
(See photograph opposite)

500 g (1 lb) scallops
½ small carrot, sliced
½ small onion, sliced
bouquet garni (comprising parsley
   stalks, bay leaf, sprig of thyme,
   a few peppercorns)
½ cup dry white wine
¾ cup of water

Mushroom duxelles:
125 g (4 oz) mushrooms,
   finely chopped
1 shallot, finely chopped
30 g (1 oz) butter
salt and freshly ground pepper

Velouté sauce:
30 g (1 oz) butter
1 tablespoon flour
¾ cup scallop stock
salt and freshly ground white pepper
1 egg yolk
1 tablespoon cream
4 tablespoons breadcrumbs
60 g (2 oz) butter

Serves: 4-6

Remove the beard from the scallops. Place remaining ingredients in a saucepan and bring to the boil, simmer gently for 20 minutes. Add the scallops and allow to poach for 5 minutes. Remove the scallops and strain the liquid.

Mushroom duxelles: Melt the butter in a pan and add the shallot. Cook for a minute and then add the mushrooms. Season with salt and pepper and cook for a further 3 minutes.

Spoon mixture into 4 scallop shells. Arrange the scallops on this Mushroom duxelles bed.

Velouté sauce: Melt the 30 g (1 oz) butter and stir in the flour. Cook for 1 minute and then add the scallop liquid gradually, stirring all the time. Season with salt and pepper and allow the sauce to cook gently for 10 minutes. Combine the egg yolk with the cream and stir into the sauce. Stir for 1 minute over the heat but do not allow the sauce to boil. Remove sauce from the heat and spoon over the scallops.

Melt butter in a pan and toss the breadcrumbs in it until they are golden and crisp. Sprinkle over the prepared scallop shells.

Place in a preheated hot oven or under the griller to heat through until golden. Serve hot, garnished with lemon wedges.

Opposite: Coquilles à la Parisienne. **Page 92:** Ratatouille (see recipe on page 106).

Grilled flounder

Australian flounder is very similar to the European sole and recipes for this fish are legion but most connoisseurs agree that grilling is the simplest and best way of cooking.

4 small flounders
pepper and salt
60 g (2 oz) melted butter
1 lemon, cut into wedges
2-4 pats maître d'hôtel butter

Serves: 4

Skin the flounders by first removing scales and fins. Make an incision in the skin only just above the tail. Insert a finger in the slit and slip it around the edges. The whole skin can then be pulled off from the tail to the head with fingers dipped in salt to prevent them slipping. Proceed the same way for the other side. Rub it over with a little pepper and salt and brush liberally with melted butter.

Have rack in grilling pan and when grill is very hot place fish on rack. Turn down heat and grill slowly 3 inches from the heat for 7-10 minutes, turning fish once. Baste with melted butter if necessary. The fish should be golden on both sides.

Serve with lemon wedges and maître d'hôtel butter.

Maître d'hôtel butter

60 g (2 oz) butter
1 tablespoon chopped parsley
squeeze lemon juice
freshly ground pepper

Cream the butter in a bowl and beat in remaining ingredients. Spoon on to a piece of foil or greaseproof paper and roll into a cylinder. Place in freezer to firm and then cut into rounds for serving.

Page 93: Salade de Campagne (Wilted salad) (see recipe on page 105).

Opposite: Salad dressings 1. Vinaigrette 2. Aïoli 3. & 4. Oil and vinegar. (see recipes on pages 116, 117).

Moules marinière

(Mussels of the sea)

2 kg (4 lb) fresh mussels
½ cup finely chopped shallots
1 clove garlic, finely chopped
bay leaf
⅔ cup dry white wine
30 g (1 oz) butter
⅓ cup chopped parsley
freshly ground pepper

Serves: 4

Wash and scrub the mussels well with a stiff brush in plenty of water. With a firm tug pull from the side of each mussel the small piece of sea-grass. Soak for 2 hours in cold water allowing them to disgorge the sand they contain.

Place in a large pan with the shallots, garlic and bay leaf, cover and cook over a brisk heat for 5 minutes or until the shells have opened. Remove the top shell from each and place in a deep serving dish, keep warm.

Taste the cooking juices and if too salty discard half. Add remaining ingredients to the pan reserving a little parsley to sprinkle on the top. Boil briskly for a few minutes to cook the shallots and to allow the sauce to amalgamate.

Pour over the mussels, sprinkle with reserved parsley and serve immediately with thick slices of crusty bread.

Serve as an entrée, or for light luncheon, doubling the quantity of mussels.

Herbed prawns

500 g (1 lb) large green prawns
125 g (4 oz) butter
2 tablespoons lemon juice
2 tablespoons freshly chopped
    parsley, dill and chives
1 teaspoon salt
freshly ground pepper

Serves: 4

Shell and devein prawns leaving tails intact. Melt butter in frying pan and when hot fry prawns gently till pink, about 3-5 minutes.

Remove pan from heat and add lemon juice and herbs. Season with salt and freshly ground pepper. Return to heat for a few moments spooning sauce over prawns. Serve hot with crusty bread.

Vegetables

Gone at last are the days when people were blase about vegetables. The tiniest plots of land are now being filled with vegetables and herbs for better eating. For instance lettuces, with no wasted outside leaves, take only a few weeks to grow and come in numerous varieties. Radishes, cucumber, capsicum and many others can be collected fresh for the making of a luncheon salad.

Greengrocers too are becoming more aware. It's easy now to obtain tiny baby marrows called zucchini or miniature new potatoes that hardly need washing.

The housewife is learning to insist she gets nothing but the best for her money and her cooking.

Individual servings of beautifully cooked vegetables make delicious entrées. Potatoes, rice and pasta go well served with the main dish as does a garnish of vegetables to perfect the dish as a whole. But why not try serving a vegetable dish separately in its own right before or after the meat dish? Salads are especially good served after the main meal, for what better way to refresh the palate after a rich dish. They are good too served on their own, perfect ingredients tossed together in a bowl to make a light meal. Remember though, the salad should be crisp so have the dressing prepared, waiting to be tossed with the salad (just enough to coat each piece) before being served. All this is just a normal part of the French way of life.

Sautéed potatoes

Potatoes for this dish should be old and fairly large. They are boiled whole first then peeled so that the wax lining of the potato is not lost.

1 kg (2 lb) old potatoes
salt
60 g (2 oz) butter
1 tablespoon oil

Serves: 4

Lightly scrub potatoes and place in a large saucepan. Cover with cold water and season with a large pinch of salt. Cover and bring to the boil. Continue boiling for 15-20 minutes or until tender, without breaking. Drain and when cooled slightly, peel.

Have ready a frying pan with melted butter and oil. Cut the potatoes into large chunks or thick slices and add to the foaming butter. Cook briskly, shaking the pan and turning the potatoes continually. They should never be left to fry. The constant turning gives the outside of the potatoes a crumbly texture, which is the delightful characteristic of this dish. Sprinkle with salt and serve immediately without draining potatoes.

Note: These potatoes go well with fish, sautéed chicken and many steak dishes.

Potatoes anna

1 kg (2 lb) old potatoes
60 g (2 oz) butter
salt

Serves: 4

Choose potatoes of medium size and uniform shape. Peel, and using a mandoline or very sharp knife, cut into wafer thin slices. Place in a colander and wash well under cold running water. Dry well in a teatowel. Place in a large bowl.

Melt butter and toss in potatoes with a large pinch of salt.

Line a thick heavy frying pan, about 18 cm (7 in) diameter with potato slices in neat overlapping circles. Continue filling pan in even circles with remaining potatoes. Place on a gentle heat and brown lightly. Use a metal spatula or knife to lift and check the potatoes are not burning. When a good colour underneath place in a preheated moderately hot oven 190ºC (375ºF) for about 30 minutes or until potatoes are tender and golden.

Place a heated serving plate on top of pan and flip over to turn out potatoes. Serve very hot.

Potatoes savoyardes

1 kg (2 lb) old potatoes
salt and pepper
grated nutmeg
1 egg, beaten
2 cups scalded milk
125 g (4 oz) grated Gruyère cheese
1 cut clove garlic
30 g (1 oz) butter

Serves: 4
Cooking time: 1 hour
Oven temperature: 180ºC (350ºF)

Peel and slice the potatoes thinly. Place in a bowl with the seasonings, beaten egg and scalded milk and 90 g (3 oz) grated cheese, combining well.

Rub shallow earthenware dish with the cut garlic clove and half of the butter. Pour in the potato mixture and sprinkle over the remaining cheese and butter cut into small pieces.

Cook in a preheated moderate oven for 1 hour or until the potatoes are tender.

Pommes mousseline

(Purée of potatoes)

These potatoes may seem like everyday mashed potatoes, and so they might be. The sieving of the potatoes and the addition of hot milk and butter make them worthy of accompanying some of the best dishes of the French cuisine.

750 g (1½ lb) potatoes
30 g (1 oz) butter
1¼ cups boiling milk
salt and pepper
pinch grated nutmeg

Serves: 4

Leaving the potatoes with their skins on place in a large pan of cold, salted water, bring to the boil and cook gently for about 20 minutes or until tender. Drain and peel the skins.

Return to the pan 2 at a time over gentle heat to dry off any moisture. Rub the potatoes through a wire sieve over the hot pan. Return the pan to a gentle heat and gradually beat in the butter and milk. Continue beating until very smooth and soft. Add the seasonings and serve as soon as possible.

Haricots vert aux oignons

(Green beans with onion)

750 g (1½ lb) green beans
60 g (2 oz) butter
1 medium onion, chopped finely
salt and freshly ground pepper

Serves: 4

Wash, top and tail the beans and if they are a little old remove the side strings. Drop into 2 cups of boiling salted water and cook, uncovered for 12-15 minutes. Drain and refresh immediately under a cold tap. Pile into a vegetable dish and keep warm.

Using the pan the beans were cooked in, melt the butter and cook the onion until browned, without burning. Season with salt and freshly ground pepper and spoon over the beans.

Carottes vichy
(Glazed carrots)

0.5 kg (1 lb) young carrots
⅔ cup water
30 g (1 oz) butter
salt to taste
1 teaspoon sugar
1 tablespoon chopped parsley
freshly ground pepper

Serves: 4

Scrape carrots and cut into thin slices. Place in a pan with water, butter, salt and sugar. Cover the pan and cook gently until tender, about 10-15 minutes.

Remove the lid from the pan and cook briskly until the liquid in the pan has completely reduced, taking care not to burn. Shake the pan frequently so that the carrots are thoroughly glazed with the sugar and butter.

Toss with the parsley and freshly ground pepper and serve piping hot.

Courgettes au beurre
(Zucchini with butter)

These tiny marrows have become quite common now that there is the demand. Cooked with butter or oil until just tender they remain slightly crisp and none of their delicate flavour is lost. They are also delicious in salads in which case they need only to be sliced and quickly blanched in boiling water, then cooked in a little good quality oil.

750 g (1½ lb) zucchini
30 g (1 oz) butter
salt and freshly ground pepper
1 tablespoon freshly chopped herbs
  (optional)

Serves: 4

Wash and top and tail the zucchini. If they are very small they can be left whole, otherwise cut into thin diagonal slices.

Drop into boiling salted water for 2 minutes.

Drain, refresh under cold water and return to pan with remaining ingredients. Cover and cook gently until tender.

Petits pois Français

(French green peas)

This is one of the best ways of preparing peas, and although so well-known, I felt they must be included in a book of French cookery.

2 kg (4 lb) fresh green peas Serves: 4
6 spring onions
1 lettuce
60 g (2 oz) butter
bouquet garni (comprising parsley
stalks, bay leaf, sprig of thyme)
2 teaspoons sugar
salt to taste
2 tablespoons water

Shell the peas and while preparing remaining ingredients, keep the peas moist by covering with a few of the shells. Peel and trim the onions. Wash the lettuce removing outside leaves and cut into quarters.

Place all ingredients in a fireproof casserole and cover with a tight fitting lid. Cover and cook over a medium heat for 30 minutes. Remove the bouquet garni and serve while fresh from the heat.

Chou au vin blanc

(Cabbage with white wine)

1 small cabbage Serves: 6
30 g (1 oz) butter
1 large onion, finely sliced
⅔ cup dry white wine or stock
salt and freshly ground pepper

Remove the outer leaves and cut the cabbage into quarters. Shred the cabbage very finely. Melt the butter in a large pan and sauté the onion until soft and light golden, about 5 minutes.

Add the cabbage, tossing well with the onion and butter. Stir frequently over a gentle heat for about 10 minutes.

Add the wine, cover with a piece of buttered paper and lid. Cook gently for 30 minutes or until tender. Season well with salt and freshly ground pepper. Serve with pork dishes.

Topinambour frits
(Deep fried Jerusalem artichokes)

This root vegetable is sometimes seen in specialty greengrocers but is common in the winter months at the fruit and vegetable markets. For identification these artichokes look similar to root ginger and are easiest peeled after cooking.

500 g (1 lb) Jerusalem artichokes   Serves: 4
4 cups salted water
juice of ½ lemon
½ cup milk
beaten egg
dried white breadcrumbs

Boil the artichokes in 4 cups salted water with the lemon juice and milk, about 30 minutes. When tender, peel them and cut into bite-size pieces. Brush with the beaten egg and coat with the breadcrumbs. Fry in hot oil until golden. Drain on crumpled paper.

Note: These are excellent served as an entrée with a home-made tomato sauce and a garnish of parsley sprigs also fried in hot oil.

Poireaux vinaigrette
(Leeks with dressing)

4-6 small leeks   Serves: 4-6
boiling salted water
½ cup vinaigrette dressing (see
   page 117)
freshly chopped herbs

Trim the leeks to about 2.5 cm (1 in) above the forking of the leaves. Split lengthwise halfway through the leek to about 5 cm (2 in) from the white bulb. Opening the leaves slightly wash well under cold running water to remove all sand and grit. Drop into boiling salted water and cook for about 10 minutes or until tender. Drain and refresh under cold water.

Arrange in a small serving dish and while still warm toss with the dressing. Chill slightly and sprinkle with the herbs before serving.

Note: A good entrée dish, especially in season when there is an abundance of leeks for then they are at their best.

Aubergines provençale

(Grilled stuffed eggplants)

2 small eggplants
salt
1 medium onion, finely chopped
2 garlic cloves, crushed
¼ cup olive oil
1 tomato, peeled and roughly
  chopped
1 tablespoon chopped parsley
salt and freshly ground pepper
⅔ cup breadcrumbs
30 g (1 oz) butter

Serves: 4
Cooking time: 25-30 minutes
Oven temperature: 190°C (375°F)

Wipe and halve the eggplants, make 1 cm (½ in) cuts in a lattice on the cut side of each. Sprinkle with plenty of salt, turn cut side down and leave to drain for 1 hour.

Wipe with a kitchen towel and scoop out the flesh. Cut into small cubes and sauté with the onion and garlic cloves in the oil until soft. Add the chopped tomato, parsley and season with plenty of salt and pepper.

Set the eggplant skins in a buttered baking dish and fill with the mixture. Sauté the breadcrumbs in the butter with remaining garlic clove. Sprinkle the eggplants with the breadcrumbs and bake in a preheated moderately hot oven for 25-30 minutes.

Salade de haricots blancs

(White haricot bean salad)

This delicious salad can be made if there are any beans left over from the Gigot à la Bretonne. Otherwise cook the beans as in the recipe on page 100, soaking them first and cooking them in water with the vegetables and seasonings; they of course aren't cooked in butter for this recipe.

2 cups cooked white haricot beans   Serves: 4-6
2 small tomatoes, peeled
   and quartered
1 tablespoon shredded black olives
1 tablespoon shredded basil
1 clove garlic, crushed
¼ cup mayonnaise
¼ cup vinaigrette dressing (see
   page 117)

In a bowl combine the beans with the tomatoes and olives. Toss with the shredded basil.

Combine the garlic, mayonnaise and vinaigrette dressing, beating until smooth and toss with the salad. Serve slightly chilled.

Salade de campagne

(Wilted salad)
(See photograph on page 93)

1 fresh young lettuce   Serves: 4
2 hard-boiled eggs
60 g (2 oz) speck bacon
2 teaspoons vinegar
freshly ground pepper
freshly chopped parsley

Wash the lettuce and dry by shaking in a kitchen cloth. If necessary tear into bite-size pieces and place in an oiled salad bowl. Roughly chop the eggs and add to lettuce.

Dice the speck and fry in its own fat until golden and the fat is transparent. Add to the lettuce with the vinegar and freshly ground pepper and sprinkle with parsley. Serve immediately while the bacon is still hot.

Ratatouille

(Vegetables cooked in oil)
(See photograph on page 92)

2 medium eggplants
salt
2 large onions, finely chopped
½ cup olive oil
2 peppers
4 zucchini
2 cloves garlic
freshly ground pepper
4 ripe tomatoes, peeled
   and quartered
freshly ground pepper
freshly chopped parsley

Serves: 4-6

Wipe the eggplants and split in halves lengthwise. Score the cut surface, about 1 cm (½ in) deep and sprinkle liberally with salt. Turn cut side down first on a plate and leave to drain, for 30 minutes

Wipe the eggplants and cut into large cubes.

Meanwhile cook the onions in the oil until soft and golden. Add the eggplants and cook a further 2 minutes. Wash and cut the peppers into fine strips and add to the pan with the zucchini which has been cut into thin diagonal slices. Add the garlic and season with freshly ground pepper. Cover and cook gently for about 15 minutes. Add the tomatoes and cook a further 5 minutes. Serve warm or chilled sprinkled with freshly chopped parsley.

Note: Serve with crusty bread or as an accompaniment to grilled meats and cold dishes.

Sauces

There seems to be no doubt about it, so often it is those exquisite French sauces that turn an ordinary dish into something magnificent.

In France sauce making is not confined to restaurants. The key to this fine art has been well-known since the time of Caréme in the late 18th century, who is considered to be the inventor of classic French cuisine.

For a sauce to be good it should be delicately seasoned so as not to take over from the dish, and fresh tasting. A sauce is best made with home made stock, which can be stored easily in the freezer. But apart from this a sauce can be made quickly and simply with ingredients on hand.

The French speak of the three mother or 'mere' sauces – brown sauce, velouté, and béchamel – and it is from these that the hundreds of French sauces stem. Brown sauce is as its name suggests, dark and rich, and is the sauce most often used for special meat dishes. Velouté is a light sauce made with a chicken, veal or fish stock. The roux of butter and flour is carefully cooked to a pale straw colour before the liquid is added. The well-known béchamel hardly needs explaining, for we all know a white sauce, but it is delicately seasoned to impart a good flavour to the dish it is added to.

Then there are the butter sauces, hollandaise, béarnaise, and the sauces that are made by adding to these. Unfortunately the fear of these sauces curdling has prevented many from making them. But they are delicious and not as difficult as they seem.

A salad is never served without a sauce or dressing in France. It isn't that their salads can't stand on their own, but a sauce is made to enhance the fresh flavours. Mayonnaise, aïoli and vinaigrette dressing are a pleasure to make and none of their fine flavour is truly captured in the purchased bottle types.

Sauce brune

(Brown sauce)

Forming the basis for so many well-known sauces, it is made with a roux of oil and flour cooked to a good russet brown. Brown jellied stock is the best for this sauce.

3 tablespoons oil
¼ cup each finely diced onion,
   celery and carrot
1½ tablespoons plain flour
2¼ cups brown stock
1 tablespoon tomato paste
bouquet garni (comprising bay leaf,
   sprig thyme, parsley stalks)
few peppercorns
salt and pepper to taste

Heat the oil in a heavy pan and cook the vegetables until softened. Blend in the flour and cook gently until a good brown, taking care not to burn the onion. Remove from the heat and add 1¾ cups stock.

Bring to the boil, stirring well and add remaining ingredients. Half cover with a lid and simmer gently for about 25 minutes. Add half the remaining stock, bring to a rapid boil. Remove from heat and remove the scum that comes to the surface.

Repeat this process with remaining ¼ cup stock. This helps to give the sauce a good, clear shine.

Strain through a fine sieve, pressing the vegetables well and reheat to use as required.

Note: A good addition to this sauce is the meat glaze set underneath the dripping poured off from a roast of beef. It keeps well refrigerated and is useful to have on hand for flavouring sauces and stews. Use about 2 tablespoons for this quantity of brown sauce.

Sauce madère

(Brown sauce with madeira)

1 quantity of brown sauce (see above)
¼ cup madeira sherry

Heat the sauce and just before serving, stir in the madeira.

Note: Serve with grilled steaks, lamb noisettes or cutlets.

Sauce veloutée

(Velvet sauce)

30 g (1 oz) butter
1½ tablespoons plain flour
1¼ cups of light stock (fish,
   chicken, veal)
salt and freshly ground white pepper
squeeze lemon juice to taste
1 egg yolk
1 tablespoon cream

Melt the butter in a pan, remove from heat and blend in the flour. Stir in the stock and slowly bring to the boil. Simmer gently for about 10 minutes and season with salt, pepper and lemon juice.

Combine the egg yolk with the cream and a little of the hot sauce. Pour back into the pan and allow to thicken slightly without boiling.

Note: Serve with fish, chicken and veal dishes.

Sauce poulette

To 1 quantity of velouté sauce (see above) made from chicken or veal stock, add 2 teaspoons finely chopped parsley and an extra squeeze lemon juice.

Note: Serve this sauce with vegetables, especially carrots and broad beans. It also goes well with boiled veal.

Béchamel sauce

1⅔ cups milk
slice of onion
few peppercorns
blade of mace (optional)
½ bay leaf
30 g (1 oz) butter
2 tablespoons plain flour
salt and white pepper

Heat milk gently with seasonings in a covered pan, about 5 minutes. Strain into a bowl and set aside.

Rinse out the pan and melt the butter, remove from heat and blend in the flour.

Stir in the milk and return to heat. Bring slowly to the boil, stirring constantly and simmer gently for 3 minutes. Season to taste and use as required.

Sauce aurore

Combine 1 quantity of béchamel sauce (see above) with ¼ cup tomato purée. Swirl in a little cream.

Note: Serve with fish, chicken, eggs and vegetables.

Sauce soubise

Finely chop 1 large onion and cook in 30 g (1 oz) butter until very soft, without colouring, in a covered pan. This should take a good 10 minutes. Add this to 1 quantity béchamel sauce (see above).

Note: A delicious sauce served with lamb, eggs and fish.

Omelette soufflé (see recipe on page 121).

Béarnaise sauce

This sauce is made on the same principle as hollandaise but has a flavoured vinegar base. Serve with steaks, fillet of beef and shellfish.

1¼ cups white wine vinegar or
    dry vermouth
1 shallot, finely chopped
few peppercorns
½ teaspoon dried tarragon
1 bay leaf
sprig thyme
2 egg yolks
125 g (4 oz) butter
1 teaspoon finely chopped parsley
freshly ground white pepper

Place the vinegar or vermouth in a saucepan, preferably enamelled, with herbs and seasonings and boil rapidly until reduced to 1 tablespoon. Put the egg yolks in a bowl and strain on the vinegar. Place over a pan of gently simmering water and whisk until thickened slightly.

Add the butter gradually by slipping it through the fingers (slightly softening it) in small pieces. Whisk until the butter is combined with the egg yolks and the sauce is thick and creamy. Stir in the parsley and season with pepper.

Sauce choron

Delicious with beef steaks or shellfish, a béarnaise sauce lightly flavoured with tomato purée, say about 1 tablespoon, and a squeeze of orange juice to taste.

Sauce paloise

Served with roast or grilled lamb or grilled chicken, it is made the same way as béarnaise with 1 tablespoon chopped mint leaves in place of the tarragon.

Almond and hazelnut gallette (see recipe on page 123).

Hollandaise sauce

This rich sauce, contrary to popular belief, can be made a little while in advance and kept ready to be heated gently in a pan of hot water before serving. This is especially useful when first learning to make it, to be sure you won't feel compelled to serve a curdled sauce to guests. It goes well with fish and vegetable dishes.

**2 egg yolks
1 tablespoon water
125 g (4 oz) butter
   (preferably unsalted)
pinch salt
squeeze lemon juice**

Place the egg yolks and water in a bowl over a pan of gently simmering water. Whisk until light and fluffy. Add the butter in small pieces gradually to the bowl, whisking well so that the sauce is always amalgamated. The more butter that is added the thicker the sauce should become. When all the butter is added and the sauce is creamy, add the salt and lemon juice to taste. The sauce should be served warm.

Tomato sauce

A freshly made tomato sauce is delicious served with fried croquettes, vegetable entrées or grilled meats and fish.

**1 kg (2 lb) ripe tomatoes
bay leaf
sprig thyme
1 small onion, thinly sliced
1 clove garlic
30 g (1 oz) butter
salt and freshly ground pepper**

Cook ingredients gently in a heavy covered pan with no water. When soft, about 10 minutes, rub through a sieve and return to pan. Swirl the butter into the sauce and season with salt and freshly ground pepper. Reheat if necessary and serve.

Cold Sauces
Mayonnaise

An extraordinary amount of mystery seems to surround the making of mayonnaise, like cooking with yeast or making a soufflé it seems to be something many cooks try to avoid. Yet making mayonnaise is one of the most relaxing and satisfying of kitchen tasks. No shop-bought mayonnaise can remotely compare with the home made variety. Just settle down in the kitchen with a bowl, wooden spoon, eggs and oil and begin making one of the most beautiful and useful sauces in the preparation of good food.

2 egg yolks
½ teaspoon salt
½ teaspoon French mustard
1¼ cups of good olive oil
2 teaspoons white vinegar

Put egg yolks, salt and mustard into a bowl. Beat vigorously with a wooden spoon until thickened. Add oil, drop by drop until ¼ cup has been added. Stir in half the vinegar. As mixture thickens add remaining oil in a thin stream. It is important to keep the consistency of the mayonnaise thick so stop every now and then to check.

When almost all the oil has been added stir in remaining vinegar and give a final beating with the last of the oil. Taste for seasoning, a grinding of white pepper and a squeeze of lemon juice may be added.

The final result will be a thick emulsion that can be used in a variety of ways.

For a coating sauce add 2 tablespoons hot water, this will also help to stabilize the mixture.

For a lighter sauce, add a spoonful of cream, milk or water, to accompany fish or cold chicken.

Tartare sauce

To 1 cup mayonnaise add 1 teaspoon each finely chopped capers, gherkins, spring onions or shallots, olives and parsley and the white of a hard boiled egg.

Note: Serve with fried fish.

Rémoulade

To one cup mayonnaise add 2 hard boiled egg yolks, finely chopped or pushed through a sieve, 1 teaspoon each chopped or crumbled tarragon, chives and capers and the whites of the eggs finely chopped.

Note: Serve with fried, crumbed pigs trotters, crumbed cutlets and hot or cold boiled meats.

Sauce verte
(Green mayonnaise)

This is made by working finely chopped mixed herbs into mayonnaise. The herbs should be chopped almost to a purée and added just before the sauce is to be served.

For 1 cup mayonnaise allow about ½ cup very finely chopped herbs – watercress, parsley, chives, tarragon or sorrel. The cress and sorrel may be blanched first by dropping into boiling water for a minute.

Drain, refresh under cold water and squeeze dry with a cloth or between two plates, before chopping and adding to the mayonnaise.

Note: Use for poached fish and hard boiled eggs.

Aïoli
(Garlic mayonnaise)
(See photograph on page 94)

This garlic flavoured mayonnaise is one of the best loved cold sauces of Provence. It is served with hot boiled potatoes, in place of butter, a few spoonfuls do wonders for hot beetroot, carrots or globe artichokes. A little may be added to the dressing for rice salads and bean salads. Boiled beef or poached chicken are livened up by a little aïoli.

Crudités (raw fresh vegetables): a selection of colourful, crisp, raw vegetables is one of the simplest and most pleasant hors d'oeuvre served with aïoli.

For 1 cup aïoli peel 4 cloves garlic and crush with the flat of a knife. Sprinkle with ½ teaspoon salt and pound to a smooth paste. Mix in a bowl with 2 egg yolks, ½ teaspoon mustard, pepper and ½ teaspoon lemon juice. Prepare as for mayonnaise, seasoning at the end with a little lemon juice in place of the vinegar.

Note: A simple way to make aïoli is to add the crushed clove garlic to the mayonnaise after it has been made.

Vinaigrette

(Oil and vinegar dressing)
(See photograph on page 94)

Vinaigrette is one of the important dressings for most salads and many other dishes. It is known throughout the world, except perhaps in France, as French dressing. Vinaigrette is a mixture of oil and vinegar, usually in the proportion of 3 parts oil to 1 of vinegar, although in France more oil is often used specially where the quality of oil is very good. It may be seasoned with mustard, garlic, chopped fresh herbs and other aromatics depending on how it is to be used.

Vinaigrette should be freshly mixed each time it is required, a soup plate and a fork is all you need, some lucky housewives own a little birch whisk which is ideal. The combination can be made in a jar and vigorously shaken. Sometimes a little bottle of oil and vinegar and the seasonings are taken to the table and the dressing mixed to suit personal tastes.

Red wine vinegar, tarragon or other herb vinegars, cider or malt vinegars may be used but as these vary in strength it is better to be light handed adding more or less to suit your taste.

1 tablespoon vinegar
¼ teaspoon salt
¼ teaspoon French mustard
freshly ground pepper
1 clove garlic
3-5 tablespoons olive oil

Put vinegar in soup bowl with salt, mustard and a good grinding of pepper. Peel garlic clove, cut into a few pieces, add to vinegar. Mix well with a fork gradually adding the oil, beating until the body of the sauce thickens slightly. Taste for seasoning. If the vinegar is too sharp a pinch of sugar will help the sauce. Remove garlic pieces.

Note: For a stronger garlic flavour the clove may be finely chopped and left in the vinaigrette.

The Stocks

A well-flavoured and shiny sauce is often the result of a good stock. The stock is made with various bones, a few vegetables to flavour and the smallest amount of seasoning. If the stock is over-seasoned it can ruin a delicate sauce. The ingredients are simmered together very gently; if allowed to boil the result will be a muddy stock, which will make a dull sauce.

Brown stock

1.25 kg (2½ lb) veal and beef bones
few peppercorns
1 cup roughly chopped onion, celery
and carrots
bouquet garni (comprising bay leaf,
parsley stalks, sprig of thyme)
½ teaspoon salt

Oven temperature: 180°C (350°F)

Wipe the bones and place in baking dish. Bake in a moderate oven until well browned, about 20 minutes. Pour off the fat and put the bones in a large pan.

Add remaining ingredients and pour in enough water to come ¾ up to the bones. Bring slowly to the boil, skim the surface. Reduce the heat and simmer gently for about 3 hours.

Strain the stock into a bowl and allow to cool before refrigerating. When the fat has set on the top remove and discard. Keep the stock well covered and use when required.

Light stock

Make as for brown stock, using veal or chicken bones. For this it is not necessary to brown the bones first. If making chicken stock the giblets, excluding the liver, are also added.

Desserts

Desserts are usually the last chapter in a cook book, not because they are of lesser importance in good eating, but because they are the refreshing grand finale to a well-planned meal.

What exquisite preparations come to mind at the mention of French desserts. Superb ice-cream confections such as the bombés and coupés or the glazed fruit pastries that hardly need to be tasted to be appreciated.

Many of the French specialities are best made on a grand scale, this is why the housewife likes to buy her pastries and cakes from the local pâtisserie.

Still there is no limit to the desserts the French make at home. Fruits are arranged in tiny pastry cases and glazed with jam, or just lightly sugared and served with a fresh cream cheese. Little pots of baked custard look superb in their china dishes, each with a different flavour.

Tarte aux pommes

(French apple tart)

Pastry:
1 cup plain flour
pinch salt
60 g (2 oz) butter
¼ cup castor sugar
2 egg yolks
few drops vanilla essence

Filling:
750 g (1½ lb) cooking apples
15 g (½ oz) butter
1 tablespoon castor sugar

Glaze:
¼ cup apricot jam
1 tablespoon water
squeeze lemon juice

Serves: 4-6
Cooking time: 30-35 minutes
Oven temperature: 190°C (375°F)

To make pastry sift flour with a pinch of salt on to a pastry board. Make a large well in the centre to form a ring. Place the remaining ingredients in the well and work them together to a smooth paste, using the fingertips of one hand. With a metal spatula gradually draw in the flour and knead lightly to form a smooth dough. Wrap and chill for at least 1 hour.

Dust pastry board with flour and roll the dough to fit a 20 cm (8 in) flan ring. Press the dough well into the sides without stretching the pastry and trim the excess. Prick the base with a fork and chill for a further 15 minutes.

To fill the flan peel, quarter and slice the apples into the flan continually levelling them. Arrange the last layer of apples overlapping in circles. Dust with the sugar and brush with the melted butter. Bake in a preheated moderately hot oven for 30-35 minutes.

After 20 minutes gently lift off the flan ring to finish cooking. Remove from the oven and brush with the glaze.

To make the glaze heat all ingredients together until clear and smooth. Rub through a sieve into a bowl and use immediately while still warm.

Note: This tart can be eaten warm or cold and is often accompanied with a bowl of freshly whipped cream.

Tarte au fromage

(Cream cheese tart)

Pastry:
**(Make up as the pastry in Tarte aux
    pommes, page 120)**

Serves: 6
Cooking time: 30 minutes
Oven temperature: 190ºC (375ºF)

Filling:
**125 g (4 oz) butter (preferably
    unsalted), softened**
½ cup sugar
250 g (8 oz) cream cheese
2 eggs
pinch ground nutmeg
sifted icing sugar

Line a 20 cm (8 in) flan ring with the pastry and chill. Cream the butter and
gradually beat in the sugar. Add the cheese, beating well until light and fluffy.
Beat the eggs gradually into the cream cheese mixture.

Turn into the uncooked pastry case, sprinkle with ground nutmeg and bake in
a preheated moderately hot oven for 30 minutes. When puffed and golden
sprinkle with icing sugar.

Note: This tart can be served hot or cold.

Omelette soufflé

(See photograph on page 111)

3 eggs
1 tablespoon sugar
2 teaspoons plain flour
1 tablespoon cream
grated lemon peel (optional)
pinch salt
15 g (½ oz) butter
2 tablespoons jam
sifted icing sugar

Serves: 2-3
Cooking time: 12-15 minutes
Oven temperature: 190ºC (375ºF)

Separate the whites from the yolks into a china or clean copper bowl.
Combine the egg yolks with the sugar, flour, cream and peel. Whip the egg
whites with the salt until stiff peaks form. Pour in the yolk mixture and fold
gently with a large metal spoon.

Heat the butter in a large omelette pan and pour in the mixture. Place in a
preheated moderately hot oven for 12-15 minutes or until golden and risen.
Slide on to a heated serving dish and spread with jam. Fold over and sprinkle
with sifted icing sugar.

Note: This omelette looks quite special with a caramelized lattice worked on
the top. To do this mark with a red-hot skewer on the sugar to burn it. Serve
immediately after decorating.

Soufflé grand marnier

45 g (1½ oz) butter
2 tablespoons plain flour
1 cup milk
¼ teaspoon salt
½ cup sugar
½ teaspoon vanilla essence
4 egg yolks
2 tablespoons Grand Marnier liqueur
5 egg whites
sifted icing sugar

Serves: 4
Cooking time: 35 minutes
Oven temperature: 180°C (350°F)

Make a band of doubled greaseproof paper about 10 cm (4 in) wide to fit around a 5 cup soufflé dish. Tie around the dish with string and brush lightly with oil. Sprinkle the inside with castor sugar, tapping it to remove any excess.

Melt the butter in a saucepan, stir in the flour off the heat and cook for 1 minute. Remove from heat and gradually stir in the milk. When smooth stir in the salt, sugar and vanilla. Return to the heat and gradually bring to the boil, stirring continuously.

When the sauce is thickened allow to cool. Stir in lightly beaten egg yolks and Grand Marnier. Beat the egg whites until very stiff and stir a spoonful into the sauce to soften the mixture. Fold in remaining egg whites with a large metal spoon lightly and quickly.

Pour immediately into the prepared soufflé dish and bake in a preheated moderate oven for 35 minutes or until well risen and golden. Dust with a little icing sugar and serve immediately.

Pêches au vin rouge
(Peaches in red wine)

4 fresh peaches
¼ cup sugar
1 cup red wine

Serves: 4

Place the peaches in a bowl and pour over boiling water to cover, leave a few seconds and remove to a bowl of iced water. The skin should now peel away easily.

Slice the peaches into 4 individual open wine glasses. Sprinkle the sugar over each. Pour ¼ cup of wine into each glass and serve as soon as possible.

Note: A crisp dessert biscuit goes well with these peaches.

Apricot mousse basque

250 g (8 oz) dried apricots
grated rind and juice of 1 lemon
2 medium apples
¼ cup sugar
3 egg whites
grated chocolate

Serves: 6

Soak the apricots overnight in cold water to cover. Drain and place in a saucepan with the rind and juice and the apples which have been peeled, cored and sliced. Add 1 cup of water and the sugar and cook gently for 15 minutes or until the fruit is soft. Drain, allow to cool and rub through a sieve. Whip the egg whites until stiff and fold quickly into the fruit purée.

Pile up in a serving dish or into individual sweet dishes and sprinkle with grated chocolate. Serve well chilled.

Note: This is a light sweet which can be made the day before.

Almond and hazelnut gallette

(See photograph on page 112)

4 egg whites
1½ tablespoons plain flour
45 g (1½ oz) ground hazelnuts
75 g (2½ oz) ground almonds
½ cup castor sugar
45 g (1½ oz) softened butter
1½ cups sliced peaches, fresh
   or canned
1½ cups cream

Serves: 6
Cooking time: 25-30 minutes
Oven temperature: 180°C (350°F)

Grease and line 3 baking sheets with greaseproof paper and mark a 20 cm (8 in) circle on each. Grease again. Set oven at moderate. Whisk egg whites until stiff and dry. Sift flour, nuts and sugar into egg whites and add butter. Gently fold mixture to combine.

Divide mixture on to baking sheets and spread out each the size of the marked circle. Place in preheated moderate oven and bake for 25-30 minutes, until pale gold. Place on wired racks to cool. To finish remove paper.

Whip cream and flavour with vanilla essence, add sugar to taste. Place one round on a dessert plate and spoon half of the cream over. Arrange sliced peaches on cream and place another round on top. Repeat with cream and peaches and place last round on top. Dust with icing sugar and decorate with extra whipped cream.

Savarin au rhum

(Yeast cake with rum)

1 cup plain flour
pinch salt
15 g (½ oz) yeast
1 tablespoon sugar
⅓ cup warm milk
2 eggs
60 g (2 oz) butter, creamed

Serves: 6
Cooking time: 25 minutes
Oven temperature: 190°C (375°F)

Syrup:
½ cup sugar
½ cup water
2 strips lemon peel
1 tablespoon rum

Sift the flour with salt into a warm bowl. Place the yeast and sugar in a small cup and allow to dissolve until liquid. Combine with the milk and beaten eggs and pour into a well in the centre of the flour. Gradually draw the flour into the yeast mixture. Beat well by hand until smooth and shiny and place the mixture into a cleaned greased bowl. Cover with a damp cloth and leave in a warm place to rise for about 1 hour.

Knock down the dough and work in the butter beating well for about 5 minutes. Butter a 20 cm (8 in) ring or savarin mould and pour in the yeast mixture. Cover and leave in a warm place for 10 minutes to prove. Bake in a preheated moderately hot oven for about 25 minutes, until golden and firm.

Meanwhile make a syrup by dissolving the sugar in the water with the lemon peel. When the sugar has dissolved bring to a boil and continue boiling for about 5 minutes. Add the rum.

Take savarin from oven and immediately pour over the syrup. Allow to stand for about 30 minutes until the syrup is completely absorbed. Turn on to a serving plate and serve with a bowl of freshly whipped cream, or pile the cream in the centre of the savarin.

Alsatian fruit torte

A delicious fruit flan with a yeast pastry base. Almost any fruit can be used, but apples, apricots and peaches are the most popular. Dried fruit is also suitable if allowed to soak until quite soft.

1 cup plain flour
a pinch salt
15 g (½ oz) yeast
1 tablespoon sugar
¼ cup warm milk
1 egg, beaten
45 g (1½ oz) butter, softened
4 apricots, halved and poached
   until tender

Serves: 4-6
Cooking time: 30 minutes
Oven temperature: 200°C (400°F)

Sift the flour with the salt into a warm bowl. Dissolve the yeast by adding the sugar and leaving for a few minutes to become liquid. Add to the milk and the beaten egg. Make a well in the flour and add the liquid ingredients and softened butter, gradually draw the flour into the yeast mixture and when all has been added beat thoroughly until smooth and shiny. Cover with a damp tea towel and leave in a warm place to rise for 45 minutes.

Prepare the fruit and leave to cool.

When the dough has risen gather together and knead very lightly. Place a 20 cm (8 in) flan ring on a baking tray and brush with melted butter and press the yeast mixture into it. Arrange the fruit over the dough and leave for a further 15 minutes in a warm place to prove.

Bake in a preheated hot oven for about 30 minutes or until a golden colour. Half way through the cooking time brush the surface with the syrup the fruit was cooked with. Delicious served straight from the oven with half-whipped cream.

Sauce sabayon aux fruits
(Sherry sauce with fruit)

2 egg yolks
1 tablespoon castor sugar
⅔ cup sweet sherry
strip of lemon peel

Put all the ingredients together in a small basin and stand it in a saucepan of simmering water. Whisk briskly until the sauce becomes thick and mousse-like. Do not allow the water to boil or the sauce will curdle the egg. Remove the lemon rind and serve immediately.

Pour over poached fruits such as pears, peaches and apricots.

Clafoutis

1 ¼ cups milk
2 eggs
1 cup flour
½ cup castor sugar
2 cups dark red cherries
60 g (2 oz) butter
1 ¼ cups cream

Serves: 4
Cooking time: 30 minutes
Oven temperature: 200ºC (400ºF)
lower to: 160ºC (325ºF)

Make a smooth batter of the milk, eggs, flour and ¼ cup of castor sugar. Add 30 g (1 oz) melted butter and mix at low speed with electric blender or beat well. Set aside in refrigerator.

Wash, stem and pit the cherries. Grease a 24 cm (9 ½ in) shallow ovenproof dish with 30 g (1 oz) butter. Sprinkle the cherries with remaining castor sugar, mix and spread over the pie plate. Pour batter over the cherries.

Bake in a preheated hot oven about 30 minutes, reducing heat to moderately slow for the last 10 minutes if necessary to prevent over-browning.

Serve at once, sprinkled with castor sugar and accompanied by cream.

Index